Handcuffs and Chain Link

RACE, ETHNICITY, AND POLITICS

Luis Ricardo Fraga and Paula D. McClain, Editors

HANDCUFFS

AND

CHAIN LINK

Criminalizing the Undocumented in America

BENJAMIN GONZALEZ O'BRIEN

UNIVERSITY OF VIRGINIA PRESS   CHARLOTTESVILLE AND LONDON

University of Virginia Press
© 2018 by the Rector and Visitors of the University of Virginia
All rights reserved
Printed in the United States of America on acid-free paper

First published 2018

9 8 7 6 5 4 3 2

Library of Congress Cataloging-in-Publication Data

Names: O'Brien, Benjamin Gonzalez, author.
Title: Handcuffs and chain link: criminalizing the undocumented in America /
    Benjamin Gonzalez O'Brien.
Description: Charlottesville: University of Virginia Press, 2018. | Series: Race, ethnicity,
    and politics | Includes bibliographical references and index.
Identifiers: LCCN 2018004850 | ISBN 9780813941325 (cloth: acid-free paper) | ISBN
    9780813941332 (e-book)
Subjects: LCSH: United States—Emigration and immigration—Government policy. |
    United States—Emigration and immigration—Political aspects. | Illegal aliens—
    United States. | Crime and race—United States. | Immigration enforcement—
    United States.
Classification: LCC JV6483 .O47 2018 | DDC 325.73—dc23
LC record available at https://lccn.loc.gov/2018004850

Cover art: US-Mexican border in Arizona. (Chess Ocampo/Shutterstock)

This book is dedicated to my mother, Frances Marie O'Brien, who believed in me even when I didn't believe in myself. This is hers as much as it is mine, and I wish she were here to share it with me.

I did it, Mom, I did it.

Thank you.

CONTENTS

Back in 2010, when I started the research for what would evolve into this book, immigration policy seemed to be headed in a positive direction. While deportations by Immigration and Customs Enforcement (ICE) had increased, the Obama administration, at least rhetorically, seemed committed to comprehensive immigration reform. The creation in 2013 of the bipartisan Gang of Eight in the Senate, tasked with coming up with a bill for comprehensive immigration reform, offered the promise of a real shift in how the United States addressed undocumented immigration. Unfortunately, it was not to be. The bill failed, and the Obama administration shifted to using executive orders to reform the approach of ICE and to normalize the status of those who had been brought to the United States as children and undocumented immigrants with US-born children under the Deferred Action for Childhood Arrivals (DACA) and Deferred Action for Parents of Americans (DAPA) programs. These executive orders were challenged by Republicans as an overreach on the part of the executive branch, which is not responsible for immigration policy, and a federal appeals court issued an injunction against the implementation of DAPA and the extension of DACA in 2015. This decision was appealed to the Supreme Court by the Obama administration, but the court deadlocked at 4 to 4 in 2016, leaving the lower court's injunction in place.

Hillary Clinton, the Democratic Party's candidate to take the reins from Barack Obama in 2017, also seemed to be committed to comprehensive reform and to share Obama's more sympathetic approach to the undocumented community. In stark contrast, Donald J. Trump, the Republican candidate, seemed like a throwback in terms of his rhetoric on immigration, reviving not only the idea that undocumented immigrants took the jobs of American workers but also, and more significantly, the notion that the undocumented posed a criminal threat to the nation. He capitalized on the shooting of Kathryn Steinle in San Francisco to argue that sanctuary policies increased crime, and he notoriously referred to Mexican immigrants as criminals and rapists. He promised to build a wall to keep America safe and force Mexico to pay for it, to freeze federal funding to sanctuary cities, and to create a "deportation force" to remove undocumented immigrants from the United States. Trump would go on to win the election, and at least in the early days of his administration he seems intent on following through on many of his promises, issuing executive orders asking that Congress approve funding for the border wall, changing the focus of ICE to all those charged with a crime but not yet found guilty, and stating that federal funds will be denied to any cities with sanctuary policies on the books. ICE appears to have become more aggressive under Donald Trump, with a number of large immigration raids occurring in the first few weeks of his presidency (Kulish, Dickerson, and Robbins 2017).

Trump's election marks a return to the rhetoric of old on undocumented immigration, with the attribution of criminality to those who in most cases have come to this country to work hard and improve their own lives and those of their families used to justify increasingly harsh treatment. Once again the symbols of undocumented immigration have become handcuffs and chain link, symbols representing internal crime control and protection from external threat. It is more important now than ever to understand how undocumented immigration became linked to notions of criminality.

The findings presented in this book underline how difficult comprehensive immigration reform will likely be and suggest that lawmakers seeking new solutions to the "problem" of undocumented immigration indeed face an uphill battle. Path dependence ensures that any deviation from criminalization will likely entail large political costs, and the critical failure of the Immigration Reform and Control Act of 1986 (IRCA) has delegitimized some of the more liberal approaches to undocumented immigration, such as amnesty, and seemingly returned immigration policy to a focus on crime-control tactics. Even under Obama, ICE deported a record number of immigrants every year through 2013, though the number decreased after that (US Immigration and Customs Enforcement 2015). Theoretically it could be said that immigration not only has converged with criminal law but now faces many of the same difficulties that accompany any attempts to shift away from the use of punishment in the treatment of crime (J. Simon 2007). As I show in the pages that follow, the rhetoric of criminality and the legal treatment of undocumented immigrants as criminals have been a part of immigration policy since Mexican immigration was first considered by Congress. The modern history of IRCA and the Illegal Immigration Reform and Immigrant Responsibility Act of 1996 (IIRIRA) further shows how difficult a shift in elite discourse and in the legal treatment of undocumented immigrants will be, particularly considering the public support for both the perception and the treatment of undocumented immigrants as criminals. After the promise of 2008, today we seem further from comprehensive immigration reform, and the undocumented are once again being portrayed as a threat to the nation, stripping them once again of their humanity. This is nothing new. In fact, it is sadly reminiscent of how Americans have dealt with undocumented immigration from the very earliest days of the nation.

This book never would have materialized without the support of Luis Fraga, Matt Barreto, and Naomi Murakawa, whose feedback, support, and assistance were invaluable in developing the ideas that would eventually become this book. I also owe thanks to all the family and friends who helped keep me sane as I worked on this project and have supported me throughout my career. Nick Fletcher deserves special mention for suggesting the book's title over drinks one night, as does my colleague Loren Collingwood, for making sure I had fifty other projects to work on when I needed a break from this one. My dogs, Maggie and Tulip (I miss you girl), snuggled with me as I wrote a great deal of this book and helped keep my anxiety at bay. I am also blessed to have my amazing and patient wife, Erica, who has always been there for me, not only as I wrote this book but also through the years I was pursuing my PhD. She has been my rock and always kept me grounded when I most needed it. Lastly, I can't forget my darling daughter, Penelope, whose giggles and goofiness always make me smile and lighten my mood, no matter how dark.

In the immortal words of the boxer Jeff Fenech, I love youse all.

Handcuffs and Chain Link

Considering Criminality

I'm not a . . . criminal. I just want to work.
—An undocumented immigrant, quoted in the *Phoenix New Times*,
October 21, 2010

When Mexico sends its people, they're not sending their best. . . . They're bringing drugs. They're bringing crime. They're rapists. And some, I assume, are good people.
—Republican presidential candidate Donald J. Trump

These quotes nicely exemplify the contradictions of undocumented immigration in the United States. On the one hand, US employers have depended on Mexican laborers since at least the end of the nineteenth century, as immigration restrictionists in Congress brought an end first to Chinese immigration and later to immigration from most of Asia, followed by reductions in immigration from southern and eastern Europe because of the Johnson-Reed Act. Despite this reliance on Mexican labor, immigrants from Mexico have regularly been the target of nativist and racist rhetoric that has painted them alternately as an economic threat because of the cheap labor they provide, a cultural threat owing to the belief that Latino communities in the United States do not assimilate in the same fashion or with the same speed as other immigrant groups, and a criminal threat because of how they entered the United States. These three threat frames have historically been used to justify stricter immigration policies not only in the United States but worldwide. Nearly every immigrant group that has come to the United States in significant numbers has at one time or another been painted as an economic, cultural, or criminal threat to the nation's citizens at some point. In the latter half of the nineteenth century, the Chinese were painted as an economic threat to American workers, with labor agitation in California leading to the Chinese Exclusion Act of 1882 (Ngai 2004). Limits on immigrants from southern and eastern European were driven in part by an argument that these groups did not assimilate as quickly as those from northern and western Europe and thus posed a threat to American culture (Tichenor 2002).

Criminality has regularly been used to argue for limits on immigration. Nativist tendencies in America led to the painting of the foreign born broadly as a criminal threat in the early years of the nation's history, though this characterization later would be linked to specific ethnic groups who were believed to be of a lesser whiteness. The immigrant-as-criminal narrative has been closely tied to race, with minority groups, both immigrant and native born, often portrayed as having greater propensities toward crime than whites. For immigrants from the Irish and the Italians to blacks, Chinese, and Mexicans, criminality has long been a justification for exclusion, fear, and the maintenance of racial segregation and hierarchies in the United States. Members of Congress have used the portrayal of immigrant groups as a "threat" to true Americans to justify racist immigration policies cloaked in the guise of guaranteeing the safety of the economy, US culture, or the public themselves. Undocumented immigrants from Mexico have been particularly easy to paint as criminals based on their method of entry. Since they are "illegal," having violated immigration policy in entering the United States, it is far easier to argue, and more acceptable in modern times, that they could break other laws while here.

In this book, I examine the early years of policy on undocumented immigration and show that the roots of the criminality frame can be traced to the 1920s and the passage of Senate bill 5094, which attached criminal penalties to undocumented immigration for the first time. Because path dependence is associated with policy making, the treatment of undocumented immigration as a crime-control issue, in both rhetoric and legislation, became locked in due to the potential costs of changing course and the feedback loops that were reinforced with each passing year. There would not be an attempt to change course until the passage of IRCA fifty-seven years later. In the period between S. 5094 and IRCA, the underlying issues driving undocumented immigration would be exacerbated by the Bracero Program and the Hart-Cellar Act of 1965. The Bracero Program, which ran from 1942 to 1965, was an agreement between the presidents of the United States and Mexico that allowed laborers to come to the United States as guest workers and offered them some protections (Ngai 2004). The number of braceros, or manual laborers, who could be brought in was too low to meet labor demands, so many employers continued to rely on undocumented labor, since there were no penalties for doing so, as employment was not considered harboring under the Texas Proviso, which was part of the extension of the Bracero Program passed in 1952 (Extension of the Bracero Program of

July 12, 1951). The Texas Proviso exempted employers from the felony charges that were now attached to harboring undocumented immigrants and ensured that there would be no consequences for the continued use of undocumented labor, which remained cheaper and easier to come by than legal braceros (Ngai 2004).

In 1965, Congress overhauled the legal system of immigration through the Hart-Cellar Act, which disposed of the national quotas that had been part of immigration policy since the passage of the Johnson-Reed Act in 1924 and revised by the Immigration and Nationality Act of 1952. Instead of country quotas, the Hart-Cellar Act imposed hemispheric quotas on immigration, with 170,000 for the Eastern Hemisphere and 120,000 for the Western. Additionally, countries in the Eastern Hemisphere were subject to an annual cap of 20,000, with those in the West initially exempted. Hart-Cellar, because of its emphasis on family reunification, helped to boost legal Mexican immigration, but it did little to address undocumented immigration. When the annual cap of 20,000 was extended to countries in the Western Hemisphere in 1976 under the Immigration and Nationality Act Amendments, legal Mexican immigration was reduced, and undocumented immigration increased as a result (Ngai 2004).

The Bracero Program shortcomings, the Texas Proviso, and the country-level cap on Mexican immigration all contributed to increasing undocumented immigration between 1929 and the passage of IRCA in 1986, placing a heavy burden on the latter, as it was the first attempt to comprehensively address undocumented immigration in the United States. The failure of IRCA to reduce undocumented immigration resulted in a return to the immigrant-as-criminal narrative and the treatment of undocumented immigration as a criminal act under IIRIRA. The congressional rhetoric of criminality and crime-control tactics to address undocumented immigration has influenced the media framing of the issue, which now relies heavily on these same tropes. Undocumented immigration is linked, both narratively and visually, to crime in many media stories, influencing how the American public thinks about this issue. Those who consume more television news content are more likely to believe that undocumented immigrants are criminals and thus to favor restrictive solutions like deportation and felony charges for the undocumented. This helps to create a feedback loop: the treatment of undocumented immigration as a crime-control issue by Congress influences media narratives, which in turn affect public opinion; public beliefs in immigrant criminality in turn help to reinforce policy making on the issue.

Criminalizing the Undocumented

In the early years of the twentieth century, immigration restriction was at its height, and hardening notions of sovereignty led to perceptions that there was a "Mexican problem" because of the porousness of the US-Mexico border. On March 4, 1929, undocumented entry was criminalized for the first time, with initial entry constituting a misdemeanor and reentry after deportation a felony under Senate bill 5094. The passage of S. 5094 in 1929 set Congress on a course that made bills like the 1996 IIRIRA, which, like S. 5094, relied on deterrence through punishment and crime-control tactics to address what is a labor issue, much more likely. The long history of regarding undocumented immigration as a criminal offense made the obvious solution one that treated it as such, as is reflected in most congressional legislation on undocumented immigration to date. This linkage in the mind of many legislators between immigration and crime helped to doom attempts at changing course to a more comprehensive, and compassionate, solution. IRCA did attempt to shift how undocumented immigration was handled by splitting legal responsibility between immigrants and employers, creating a guest-worker program, and allowing certain segments of the undocumented population to apply for amnesty. When IRCA's changes failed to "solve" undocumented immigration, the response was to return to the policies the United States had relied on for the fifty-seven years between the initial criminalization in 1929 and the passage of IRCA: more deterrence through punishment, increased border patrol, greater militarization. IRCA represented what I term a *critical policy failure,* a failed attempt to shift policy that results in regression to and reinforcement of the previously existing path.

Yet just examining the legislative history of the criminalization of undocumented immigration tells us little about its effect on one of the drivers of congressional legislation, the American voter. Therefore, I also examine what predicts a belief in immigrant criminality among the American public and the effect this belief has on policy preferences. Media framing of undocumented immigration has been found to be largely negative, with Kim et al. (2011) finding that newspaper coverage between 1997 and 2006 tended to rely on the criminality frame more frequently than any other. Like congressional rhetoric, the media tend to frame undocumented immigration as a crime-control issue, which likely has an effect on public opinion.

Path Dependence, Critical Policy Failures, and the Legacy of S. 5094

In *Logics of History* (2005) William H. Sewell Jr. details the significance of time in the study of social transformations. Sewell argues that individual events, defined as "brief and intense sequences of social interactions that have long-lasting effects on the subsequent history of social relations," have an impact on social interactions (2005, 271). For Sewell, past events are crucial to understanding social transformations because they provide the catalyst for change. Events lead to a change in the very structure of society and thus affect all future social interactions, as well as the nature of societal structures. Events can challenge or even undo the most durable of historical trends, but they can also reinforce existing ones (2005, 102). There had long been a suspicion that the foreign born had a propensity to criminality but there had been no linkage between the rhetoric and the legal treatment of these groups until the passage of S. 5094, which would significantly alter the social structure regarding undocumented immigrants, formally making them Ngai's "impossible subjects," those who are part of the nation but also forever separate from it (Higham 1994; Ngai 2004).

In addition to transforming social structures and norms, events like the passage of S. 5094 can also drive future political choices, with politics comprising a number of processes that are path dependent (Pierson 2004). For these processes, small events early on may have a larger impact than large events at a later stage because of the importance of sequencing. Path dependence assumes that changes that occur early in a process result in positive feedback and further movement in the same direction. Making one choice at one point in time constrains future choices in some way. Even if the choice made does not necessarily cut off other options, positive feedback loops usually make it easier to continue down the road chosen than to reverse the original decision (Pierson 2000, 2004; Thelan 1999). In terms of Mexican immigration, the decision in 1929 to criminalize undocumented immigrants rather than their employers shaped all future policy decisions. Undocumented immigration was to be dealt with through punishment of the immigrant while turning a blind eye to the profits being made from their labor by US employers.

Path dependence in the post-IRCA period can be understood by looking at critical policy failures (CPFs). As stated above, CPFs are pieces of legislation that attempt to significantly shift policy approaches but fail to produce the desired effect, in the case of IRCA a reduction in un-documented immigration. However, because they represent such a large departure from the policies of the past, their failure leads to a regression to and reinforcement of the previously existing path. CPFs are missing from theories of path dependence, which assumes movement in the same direction until moments of punctuated equilibrium open windows of opportunity for change. Path dependence theory does not account for pieces of policy that attempt a shift away from an existing path but whose failure instead leads to a regression and reinforcement of it.

IRCA shifted the US approach toward undocumented immigration through the creation of the first amnesty program for undocumented immigrants and an attempt to levy fines on employers. Under IRCA all immigrants who had continuously resided in the United States before January 1, 1982, could apply for legalization. Both the Replacement Agricultural Worker (RAW) and Seasonal Agricultural Worker (SAW) programs were set up to meet labor demands. Finally, employers were required to attest to the immigration status of their employees and faced a fine if they were found to be knowingly hiring or recruiting undocumented immigrants (Immigration Reform and Control Act of 1986; Tichenor 2002). This was an significant departure from past attempts to control undocumented immigration, not only in the comprehensive approach it took but also in its conceptualization of the immigrants themselves, who were no longer characterized as criminals. However, when IRCA failed to stop the flow of undocumented immigration, it became a CPF and created a boomerang effect in US policy, with a swift shift back to, and a reinforcement of, criminalization through IIRIRA. Aside from IRCA, congressional action on undocumented immigration has been characterized by relatively few attempts at comprehensive reform, on the one hand, and a tendency to respond to undocumented immigration through criminalization and militarization of the border, on the other.

In many ways immigration control mirrors crime control and the "severity revolution" detailed by Jonathan Simon (2001). Once deterrence through punishment became the norm, few politicians wanted to attempt a return to rehabilitation because of the potential high cost to their political career. Since a large percentage of the American public believe that undocumented immigration is in and of itself a crime, few politicians have an incentive to pursue immigration reform that does not in some way increase detention, deportation, and criminal penalties. Criminals, or those believed to be criminals, receive little sympathy from political groups in America, and therefore both crime-prevention programs and immigration policy are hard to overhaul. The lack of sympathy for undocumented immigrants also makes undocumented migration a politically fraught topic, one that it is easier to avoid or toe the line on.

New social initiatives tend to entail large start-up costs, so there are incentives to work within the existing system, which currently emphasizes enforcement and deterrence (Pierson 2004). Once a particular policy path is chosen, there are learning effects: people are taught how to operate under the existing system, and innovations are likely to be developed for the existing system. There are also adaptive expectations because of one choice triumphing over another. The path not taken becomes less appealing as a result of losing out. This makes individuals more likely to prefer a path that has already been successful to ones that have failed; since IRCA represented a CPF, a return to criminalization became probable (Pierson 2001, 2004; Thelan 1999). Control of undocumented immigration is a difficult problem requiring a solution that addresses both push and pull factors, in many cases an entirely new approach would be necessary. When IRCA came up short, there was a quick return to the far simpler criminalization that had been the norm of US immigration policy. Elites frame an issue in a way that typically presupposes its solution, so when the criminality frame was revived following the failure of IRCA, solutions linked to crime control were once again favored. Another example is car accidents. In the 1980s car accidents were framed as an issue of drunk driving, leading to increasing penalties for individuals who drove under the influence, while other causes of car accidents were ignored (Gusfeld 1981). Deborah Stone (1989) argues that this is the case for a host of social problems and that the choice of framing is often a strategic one that favors a given course of action. Prior to IRCA undocumented immigration had largely been framed as a crime-control issue, though IRCA tried to reframe it as a labor issue instead. When the comprehensive reform attempted by IRCA did not stem the tide of undocumented immigration, politicians revived the less politically costly criminality frame. Even if crime-control tactics did not work, they allowed politicians to look "tough on crime," a stance that had become increasingly appealing beginning in the late 1960s (J. Simon 2001, 2007).

Punctuated Equilibrium, IRCA, and the Return to the Path Most Traveled

Many policy areas demonstrate *punctuated equilibrium,* long periods of stability followed by windows for possible shifts, often driven by external events (Baumgartner and Jones 1993). Until the 1920s, policy on Mexican immigration had been largely to ignore it, allowing the number of Mexican immigrants to be regulated by the market (Ngai 2004). Three things led to the opening of a window for change in policy in regard to unregulated immigration from Mexico. First, immigration restrictionists succeeded in limiting European immigration in 1924, a longtime goal. This led to a focus on Mexican immigration, which had received little attention on the part of Congress prior to the passage of Johnson-Reed. Second, the end of World War I in 1918 began to harden notions of state sovereignty and made the unregulated southern US border impossible to maintain in an era when land borders were increasingly seen as physical boundaries that required strict regulation (Ngai 2004). The formation of the Border Patrol in 1924 for the first time allowed for the pursuit and apprehension of undocumented immigrants (Ngai 2003). Finally, the start of the Great Depression in 1929, like most economic downturns, led to increased nativism (Higham 1994). The Great Depression helped drive perceptions of economic threat from immigrant groups and helped shift the attention of the American public onto Mexican immigration as a source of potential danger to their economic well-being.

Baumgartner and Jones (1993, 6) state that "every interest, every group, every policy entrepreneur, has an interest in establishing a monopoly—a monopoly on political understandings concerning the policy of interest, and an institutional arrangement that reinforces that understanding." The success of immigration restriction in 1924, the beginning of the Great Depression in 1929, and hardening notions of state sovereignty all helped to dismantle the previous construction of Mexican immigration as a matter of labor demands regulated by the market. These external events constructed Mexican immigration as a law-and-order issue, and undocumented crossing was reborn as a criminal act in congressional rhetoric, beginning the now longstanding association of undocumented immigrants with criminality. No longer was undocumented Mexican immigration about labor demands; it was now about threats to the very security, culture, and economy of the country. S. 5094 reflected this new construction, allowing for a demonization of undocumented immigrants as criminals and as a result placing the burden of responsibility on the immigrant rather than on the employer, which allowed for continued access to cheap labor for economic interests in the United States.

Because of the competing interests of restriction and access to labor, Mexican immigration came to be handled in two ways. Legal Mexican immigration saw a relative lack of restriction due to resistance by labor interests, with even requirements like head taxes waived during times of labor shortages (Ngai 2004; Tichenor 2002). Illegal Mexican immigration, on the other hand, was dealt with through apprehension, detention, criminal charges, and deportation of the immigrant, while the employer faced no sanctions. Businesses continued to rely on undocumented immigrant labor without penalty, and the undocumented population had little recourse in the case of mistreatment (Ngai 2004). This arrangement satisfied the two important interests in the immigration policy arena in the early part of the nation's history: employers who were reliant on Mexican labor and restrictionists who sought to reduce the overall flow of Mexican immigration.

Had many American industries not relied on Mexican labor, quotas might have been extended to Mexico during this period, but as I show in chapter 1, there was heavy resistance to quotas on the part of agriculture interests. The resistance of agriculture and business interests to the restriction of Mexican immigration has been cited as one of the reasons why US immigration policy never became as restrictive as it might have (Tichenor 2002). Yet this resistance rarely benefited the undocumented migrants themselves, who were ignored in the best of times and actively hunted down for deportation during the worst of times. Unable to restrict the legal immigration of Mexicans, restrictionists such as the Southern Democrats John Box of Texas and Coleman Blease of South Carolina thus turned their eyes toward the criminalization of the long-standing practice of unregulated crossing in 1929. In the same year that S. 5094 passed, the Immigration and Naturalization Service instituted a campaign of "Mexican Repatriation," which sought to use the threat of raids, deportations, and penalties to force Mexican immigrants (both legal and illegal) to return to Mexico. Both actions were the culmination of increasing hostility toward Mexican immigration throughout the 1920s, as is well documented (Hoffman 1974; Ngai 2004; Tichenor 2002).

The passage of S. 5094 in 1929 led to a fifty-seven-year period in which there was almost no comprehensive congressional action on undocumented immigration. The Bracero Program, the exemption of employers from charges of harboring in 1952, and the country-level quotas for Mexico established by the amendments to the Hart-Cellar Act in 1976 all did little to address undocumented immigration and in fact helped to exacerbate some of the problems that contributed to it. Not until 1986 would there be another moment of punctuated equilibrium, with Congress once again specifically taking up the issue of undocumented immigration. This attention to undocumented immigration and window for policy change was again the result of several converging factors. First was the election in 1980 of Ronald Reagan, who saw open borders and a free-trade zone that included people as well as goods as the solution to undocumented immigration (Tichenor 2002). Second was increasing media and public attention to the issue of undocumented immigration, which forced Congress to act (Tichenor 2002). Finally, the divided Congress in 1986, with Democrats controlling the House and a Republican Senate, made compromise on immigration a necessity. IRCA represented a rare opportunity to change course, a moment of punctuated equilibrium in which policy change was possible and a new path for immigration policy might be created. As I detail in chapter 2, IRCA would come to represent a critical failure, ultimately leading to a revival of the criminality frame, the passage of IIRIRA in 1996, and a return of the policy monopoly that had existed since 1929.

While criminality has been a part of congressional rhetoric on immigration, it is unclear whether the same notions of immigrant criminality are held by the American public and how they affect policy preferences. Whether perceptions of criminality lead to support for various solutions to undocumented immigration is also unclear. If we are to pursue comprehensive immigration reform, we must be aware of public perceptions of undocumented immigrants and how these affect with policy preferences. I look at the role of public perceptions in chapters 3 and 4.

Perceived Threat and Immigration

While there has been little research on perceptions of immigrant criminality specifically, there has been a great deal of research on the impact of the perceived economic and cultural threats from immigration on public opinion. A study conducted in the Netherlands found that perceptions that immigrants posed a threat to Dutch cultural identity led to higher levels of hostility toward immigrants and greater favorability for immigration restriction (Sniderman, Hagendoorn, and Prior 2004). While perceptions of cultural threat were most likely to lead to hostility, beliefs that immigrants posed an economic threat to the nation were also significant, and collective threats were found to elicit greater hostility than did threats to the individual.

Individuals have also reported more prejudice when they were asked to identify interpersonal differences between their group and Mexican immigrants (Zarate et al. 2004). When immigrants were seen as differing from the norm, they were believed to pose a threat to the social fabric of the country and were subsequently regarded more negatively. Other research has assessed the effects of both *realistic* and *symbolic* threat per-

ceptions on prejudice against immigrants. Symbolic threats are conceptualized as threats to national culture or values, while realistic threats,
drawing on the work of Lawrence Bobo, are seen as threats to the economic, social, or political resources of whites (Bobo 1983, 1988, 1999;
Bobo and Hutchings 1996). Both symbolic and realistic threats were
found to have an effect on prejudice toward immigrants, suggesting that
perceived economic, cultural, and criminal threats influence how individuals react to immigrant groups and thus the importance of examining
the predictors of these beliefs (Stephan, Ybarra, and Bachman 1999). Another study found that immigrant groups were viewed most negatively
when they were believed to pose both realistic and symbolic threats to
one's own group, which fits neatly with psychological findings regarding
in-group/out-group bias (Stephan et al. 2005).

Similarly, Canadian students who were provided with positive or negative descriptions of a fictional immigrant group were found to react to
the physical relevance of the immigrant group to the respondent and
the descriptions they received (Maio, Esses, and Bell 1994). Individuals expressed higher levels of prejudice if they believed the immigrants
were moving into their own province and if they had received a negative
description of the group, emphasizing the importance of realistic threat
perceptions. A further pair of studies in Canada manipulated the economic threat posed by immigrants. In the first study, participants were
led to believe that the immigrant group would be a strong competitor
for scarce jobs, while in the second the immigrant group was portrayed
as having high levels of success in a difficult economic climate. In both
studies, the authors found that high levels of realistic threat generated
greater expressions of prejudice toward the fictitious immigrant group
(Esses et al. 2001; Esses, Jackson, and Armstrong 1998). These findings
suggest that perceptions of threat lead to greater expressions of prejudice,
and not vice versa (Stephan et al. 2005, 3; Stephan, Ybarra, and Bachman 1999).

Perceptions of group threat have been shown to be accurate predictors
not only of negative affect toward the target group but also of preferences
for immigration restriction. A study of public attitudes toward immigration in the United States, France, and Germany found that perceived
cultural or economic threats from immigrant groups increased opposition to immigration in all three countries, despite significant differences
in culture, history, and experience with immigration (Fetzer 2000). Further evidence for these finding was found in a 2001 study of the impact
of group threat on immigration attitudes (Wilson 2001). In this study,

Thomas Wilson notes that "native-born Americans' opposition to policies benefiting immigrants is based on their perceptions that immigrants pose a direct threat to their interest" (495). Research thus suggests that perceptions of immigrant threat play a central role in determining policy preferences, but nearly all the work to date focuses exclusively on cultural or economic threats, while Luis Fraga points out that criminality among the undocumented is one of the arguments regularly trotted out in support of stricter immigration policy (Fraga 2009).

Media and Perceived Threat

Another reason why we know very little about what is likely to drive perceptions of criminal threat is that the question is not included in most surveys on immigration attitudes. While questions about the economic or cultural threat posed by undocumented immigrants are common, few surveys ask about perceived criminality. Based on the characterization of Latinos in news stories in the United States, it is very possible that media consumption would be a strong predictor of belief in the immigrant-as-criminal narrative. Legislation tends to attract public and media attention to immigration, which is often a secondary concern of the American public. Research examining newspaper coverage of Arizona's SB1070 between February 23 and June 23, 2010, found that most of the articles were published following passage of the bill in April 2010, suggesting that the controversy surrounding the bill attracted greater media attention to the immigration debate (Chavez, Whiteford, and Hoewe 2010). Google Trends also showed a doubling in search interest for immigration-related stories between April 20 and April 30, 2010, immediately preceding and following passage of Senate bill 1070. Both findings suggest that elite attention to issues like undocumented immigration tends to drive media coverage. In an examination of how Latinos are portrayed in American media, Leo Chavez (2008) argues that Latino immigrants are regularly portrayed as different from other immigrant groups, with a focus on what he terms the "Latino Threat Narrative." This narrative characterizes Latinos as unwilling or unable to assimilate into American culture and therefore a threat to the dominant culture in the United States. It also portrays Latino immigrants as criminals who drain social services and are an invading force.

Domke, McCoy, and Torres (1999) found that media stories could prime subjects to focus on some aspects of immigration instead of others and that this influenced their assessment of immigration's impact on the United States. When individuals were primed to think in material terms by having immigration presented in terms of economics, expedience, tangible resources, and practicality, they were less likely to believe that it would have a positive impact on the US economy. In addition, the material frame also activated racial perceptions and linked them to political judgments, so that perceptions of Latinos as violent led to a greater desire to reduce current immigration levels. This was not the case when immigration was framed in ethical terms. Domke and his colleagues concluded that these findings showed the direct impact that media stories and framing have on immigration attitudes. The portrayals of Latino immigrants in the media are therefore likely to have an impact on threat perceptions as well as immigration policy preferences, and past studies have shown that the media tend to feature images of Latino immigrants being arrested in stories on immigration (Drier and Tabak 2009).

Immigrant Criminality

While there is ample evidence of perceived economic and cultural threats from undocumented immigration, and while it is believed that these threats tend to lead to more restrictive preferences in regard to immigration, there is no evidence to date on the criminal threat frame. What proportion of the American public believes this frame? Does it have an effect on policy preferences?

Proponents of Proposition 187 in California used the criminal threat frame in pushing for its passage in 1994, with one portion of the bill stating that the people of California "have suffered and are suffering personal injury and damage caused by the criminal conduct of illegal aliens in this state." In *The New Nativism*, Robin Dale Jacobson (2008, 47) states, "The struggle over Proposition 187 was a critical modern moment criminalizing Mexican migration. During the campaign, proponents connected notions of danger and criminality with the act of undocumented migration through race. What had been a discrete act of violating immigration law became, in the eyes of the measure's supporters, a criminal tendency in Mexicans." Notions of criminality were attached to the race of the individual rather than to the act of illegal crossing, painting Latino immigrants as having a predisposition to crime more generally. A bill that was under consideration in Florida mirrored Arizona's SB1070 but was explicit in its racial profiling by exempting citizens of thirty-two European nations, Canada, and four Asian countries from having to produce anything beyond a passport to prove that they were in the United States legally, though ultimately this did not pass (Elfrink 2010).

During his presidential campaign, Donald Trump very explicitly called undocumented Mexican immigrants rapists and criminals, while at the same time pledging to build a wall along the southern US border to keep these individuals out. Although there is no evidence for Trump's claim, it no doubt had a reinforcing effect on nativism and the perceptions of criminality already held by the American public. These perceptions of criminality and of undocumented crossing as a criminal violation are important because they link immigration with law and order in the minds of Americans. Research has shown that law-and-order concerns and out-group bias influenced whether individuals believed that undocumented immigrants should receive humanistic treatment. This out-group bias was based on race rather than nationality, with Canadian immigrants ranked more highly on the humanistic-treatment scale than Latino immigrants, even though both had committed the same violation (Lee and Ottati 2002). Thus, a group of immigrants who are believed to be criminals, or to have tendencies toward criminal behavior would be predicted to elicit a negative reaction in terms of treatment, which is in turn tied to policy.

The Literature So Far and the Questions Ahead

Chapter 1 analyzes the congressional debate on the Johnson-Reed Act and S. 5094, arguing that the passage of the latter represented the culmination of increasing administrative actions aimed at Mexican immigration and increasing concerns about undocumented immigration that began in 1924. I also argue that this piece of legislation marked the beginning of the convergence between immigration and criminal law that scholars today refer to as crimmigration. Further, I show that the rhetoric on Mexican immigration during this time differs little from the modern rhetoric of this debate, providing further evidence that if we want to find the roots of the criminal threat frame, we must look all the way back to the 1920s. All the threat frames associated with undocumented Mexican immigration today were part of the rhetoric in these early congressional debates, and S. 5094 gave legal weight for the first time to these nativist and racist perceptions of immigrant criminality.

   Chapter 2 moves from 1929 to the 1980s and 1990s with an analysis of congressional debate on IRCA and IIRIRA. I find that the criminality frame was downplayed in debate over IRCA, especially in the Senate, while the economic contributions of undocumented immigrants were emphasized in a way they had not been in debate on Johnson-Reed or S. 5094. A number of factors led to a moment of punctuated equilibrium in the mid-1980s that opened a space for a shift in policy away from the path of criminalization that had dominated the US response to undocumented immigration up to that point. This shift is reflected in the change in congressional rhetoric on IRCA, which focused on a more balanced approach to undocumented immigration that addressed both push and pull factors for the first time. IRCA attempted a comprehensive approach to immigration and moved away from treating undocumented immigration simply as a crime-control issue by acknowledging the responsibility of employers while also trying to address the labor needs that drove undocumented immigration. IRCA also introduced the only amnesty program for undocumented immigrants in US history.

Yet because of the broad reforms it attempted, IRCA carried a heavy burden, and its shortcomings were later cited as a repudiation of more liberal immigration policies. It represented a CPF that resulted in a return to the previous policy approach that treated undocumented immigrants as criminals and even reinforced it, as is reflected in the passage of IIRIRA in 1996. The rhetoric of criminality returned in the debate on IIRIRA, where it was much more common than in any of the other pieces of legislation I examined. Chapter 2 lays out my argument that the failure of IRCA led to a return to and reinforcement of the immigrant-as-criminal narrative, which would see a massive resurgence in the 1990s not only in federal legislation but also in state-level legislation like California's Proposition 187. The passage of IIRIRA led to a return to the previous policy path on undocumented immigration, where it was constructed as a criminal violation and crime-control tactics were the solution.

In Chapter 3 I turn from a consideration of path dependence, policy, and elite rhetoric to a functional examination of beliefs in immigrant criminality among the American public. To date, no studies have examined perceptions of immigrant criminality in detail; most public-opinion studies focus on the economic and cultural threat frames instead. To examine public opinion on the immigrant-as-criminal narrative, I draw on two surveys that included questions about perceptions of immigrant criminality. Those surveyed were asked whether they believed that undocumented crossing was a crime and immigrants were therefore criminals; that undocumented immigrants were more likely to be involved with drugs and gangs; and lastly, that undocumented immigration increased crime rates. Both surveys also included an oversample of blacks, allowing me to examine differences in perceptions of criminality between whites and blacks in the United States. This is important for many reasons, not the least being that if little is known about public perceptions of immigrant criminality, even less is known about how this varies among racial groups. In addition, blacks have themselves regularly been painted as a criminal threat in both media and elite rhetoric (Entman 1990, 1994; Mendelberg 2001; Russell-Brown 1998; Welch 2007). Thus it might be asked whether this makes them less likely to believe these same claims when they are leveled at different groups. The criminal threat frame for whites is unique among the various frames in that it is the only one affected by consumption of television news.

Finally, in chapter 4 I examine the effect of criminal threat perceptions on policy preferences of both blacks and whites. I argue that perceptions of criminal threat should increase support for deportation and felony charges for all undocumented immigrants while decreasing support for a pathway to citizenship. What I find is that a belief that crossing is a crime is associated with increased support among whites for deportation and felony charges, while criminal threat played no role in policy preferences among blacks. This suggests that different criminal threat frames will resonate with different segments of the American public.

ONE

From Open Borders to Locked Doors

In 1929, riding on the success of immigration restriction in 1924 through the Johnson-Reed Act and increasing hostility toward Mexican immigrants, Congress passed Senate bill 5094, also known as the Undesirable Aliens Act, which attached penalties to undocumented immigration and criminalized reentry after deportation, making it a felony.

In this chapter, I argue that legislation in the 1920s, culminating in the passage of S. 5094 in 1929, set the convergence of immigration and criminal law in motion by explicitly linking undocumented immigration and crime legally. Before this time such linkages had existed in the rhetoric on immigration, which lacked the weight of law, but S. 5094 formalized the linkages between immigration violations and crime, making increasing criminalization more likely (Pierson 2000, 2004; Sewell Jr. 2005; Thelan 1999). Until IRCA was passed in 1986, the Undesirable Aliens Act was one of the few pieces of congressional legislation that specifically addressed undocumented immigration, the only real exception being the "Wetback Bill" of 1952, also known as the Immigration Act of March 20th, 1952, which made it a felony to smuggle in undocumented immigrants or conceal them. This did, somewhat conspicuously, omit employment as a form of concealment.

In the following pages, I detail the evolution of US policy on undocumented immigration from the Johnson-Reed Act of 1924, the first major piece of immigration legislation in the twentieth century, to the passage of S. 5094, which attached criminal penalties to undocumented immigration for the first time. I argue that criminalization likely increased because of the increasing problematization of Mexican immigration in the 1920s and the passage of S. 5094, as successive Congresses came into session in a climate in which the major tools used to address undocumented immigration were those frequently associated with crime control, resulting in a rhetoric that painted Mexican immigrants as "illegals." This tendency to treat undocumented immigration as a criminal act was linked to a longstanding tradition in American politics of viewing the foreign born as generally predisposed to criminality (Higham 1994; Zolberg 2006).

Criminality as Racial Project

Before beginning a discussion of immigrant criminality, it is important to acknowledge that this is part of the larger American racial project. Rogers Smith argues that one of the traditions that shaped our nation was an ascriptivist one based on the belief that "true Americans are in some way 'chosen' by God, history, or nature to possess superior moral and intellectual traits, often associated with race of gender" (Smith 1993, 563). Ascribing to nonwhites negative traits like criminality or immorality made it possible to exclude them from the state, either through denial of citizenship or through slavery and Jim Crow. Citizenship would be limited to whites until 1866, when it was extended to blacks as well, but nonwhite immigrants would not be able to naturalize until passage of the McCarran-Walter Act in 1952. Control over America's cultural identity had long been linked to immigration, with a high premium placed on maintaining racial purity (Zolberg 2006). Even the Irish were characterized as being of a lower racial stock and a threat to racial purity, which was one of the motivations for limiting their immigration through the Johnson-Reed Act.

Criminality was not a stereotype limited to the undocumented; it had been assigned to various racial and ethnic groups earlier in American history to justify denying them rights enjoyed by "true" Americans. Painting nonwhites as criminals justified their social control and segregation, as well as acts of preemptive violence in the name of safety for whites. Criminality is still used today to justify the social control of blacks in the United States, as Michelle Alexander documents in *The New Jim Crow: Mass Incarceration in the Age of Colorblindness*. Alexander argues that modern crime control and the war on drugs are ways of maintaining racial caste systems established under slavery and, later, Jim Crow. She acknowledges that her book deals specifically with the treatment of blacks in the US criminal-justice system and that "little is said here about the unique experience of women, Latinos, and immigrants" (Alexander

2010, 16). Notions of black criminality, today used to justify mass incarceration and the excesses of the drug war, have their roots in the earliest years of the nation's history, in the belief in white superiority and personhood that led to the creation of America's racial caste system. Similarly, institutional claims of criminality attributed to undocumented immigrants have shaped the modern experience and treatment of Latinos, immigrant or otherwise. As Ngai (2004) details in *Impossible Subjects: Illegal Aliens and the Making of Modern America,* the construction of the "illegal immigrant" was used as a way of controlling nonwhite immigrant populations; in the case of Mexicans this meant retaining access to their physical bodies for the purposes of labor but treating them as criminals when this labor was no longer needed. Regarding the undocumented as criminals justifies their exclusion from the nation and their treatment as a group who must be controlled. These negative associations are nothing new, nor are they unique to undocumented immigrants, but the undocumented and blacks are alone in seeing these associations of criminality endure, both in rhetoric and policy, to this day.

Immigrant Criminality in Historical Context

The foreign born had long been suspected as being more inclined to crime. Some of these suspicions may have stemmed from the use of transportation from Great Britain as a means of punishment for crimes committed, particularly religious or ideological crimes, such as those related to anarchist or communist activities, but they were also undeniably linked to ethnicity and race (Kanstroom 2007; Zolberg 2006). By the twentieth century, this belief was relatively engrained in public opinion, with the Irish and Italians specifically painted as potential criminals (Higham 1994). There was enough concern about immigration, including the potential criminality of the foreign born, that a joint House and Senate commission was formed to examine whether immigration posed a threat to the United States. The commission, officially the United States Commission on Immigration, was nicknamed the Dillingham Commission, after William Paul Dillingham, the Vermont senator tasked with leading it. The commission would eventually produce forty-two volumes examining different aspects of the immigration question, making it the first comprehensive examination of immigration in US history (Tichenor 2002). The thirty-sixth volume specifically examined the question of immigrant criminality, and it is worth analyzing some of its findings, as these would play a role in shaping immigration policy in the United States broadly and the Johnson-Reed Act of 1924 in particular.

The Dillingham Commission did not have the data necessary to examine differences in crime rates because of immigration or even differences in crime rates nationally between immigrants and the native born. Instead it concerned itself with how the character of crimes committed had changed because of immigration, drawing on data from five different sources, data which largely covered urban areas and a limited number of geographic regions. The report drew on documents from the New York City magistrates' courts, the New York Court of General Sessions, the New York County and Supreme Court, the Chicago Police Department, and Massachusetts prisons. In its analysis of changes in the character of crime, it divided offenses into five different categories: gainful offenses, or crimes against property; offenses of personal violence; offenses against public policy, such as public drunkenness; offenses against chastity, such as prostitution; and unclassified offenses (US Commission on Immigration 1911). The figures reported by the commission were only for arrests, which is one reason why the report did not specifically address whether immigrants were responsible for more crime than the native born. (A later report on immigrant criminality by the National Commission on Law Observance and Enforcement, also known as the Wickersham Commission, in 1931 would discuss some of the problems with using arrest rates alone as an indicator of increased criminality, as immigrants might simply be more likely to be arrested.) In addition, the geographic limitations of the Dillingham Commission report also led to some questions of the generalizability of its findings, because only statistics from New York, Massachusetts ,and Illinois were available, with no data from the South or the West Coast.

The findings of the Dillingham Commission did seem to support existing beliefs in immigrant criminality, particularly as they related to national groups such as Italians. In general terms, the commission did find some differences between the native born and immigrants in terms of the numbers arrested for the five categories of crime the report examined. Gainful offenses were far more common for those born in the United States than for immigrants (US Immigration Commission 1911, 38). They accounted for one-tenth of all crimes by the native born but only one-sixteenth of those by the foreign born. Interestingly and somewhat unsurprisingly, the crimes committed by second-generation descendants of immigrants resembled those committed by the native born more than they did those committed by immigrants, with a greater number of gainful offenses and a smaller number of crimes of personal violence. Even in regard to the much-vilified Italians, the report states, "Striking illustration of this is afforded by the Italian second-generation group, in which the relative frequency of the various classes of crime is quite unlike that of the Italian immigrant group" (US Immigration Commission, 1911, 70). This suggests that the criminality in question was reduced via assimilation in as little as one generation, making second-generation national groups virtually indistinguishable from the native born.

As with gainful offenses, there were differences between the native born and immigrants when it came to crimes of personal violence, with a higher number of immigrant offenders. The number of crimes against public policy was higher among immigrant groups, while there was no clear relationship between nativity and crimes of chastity. It is worth considering whether these relationships hold even when the crimes composing each category in the commission report are disaggregated. The personal-violence category is helpfully broken down into five subcategories: kidnapping or abduction, simple assault, violent assault, homicide, and rape. Of those arrested, on average a higher percentage of immigrants than of native born were arrested for simple and violent assault and homicide. There was some variation, though, with New York City magistrates' courts showing identical or near identical numbers for both types of assault and homicide, though the report stressed that these findings only held in the case of data from the magistrates' courts (US Immigration Commission 1911, 42). But the variation between the statistics from the New York City magistrates' courts and the other statistics in the study should be a red flag. There may have been variation in crime rates based on geographic location, and the study is quite limited in this respect, since it only utilizes data from New York, Chicago, and Massachusetts.

The report also examined crime by ethnicity and race, and its findings were particularly scathing when it came to Italians. "The increase in offenses of personal violence in this country is largely traceable to immigration from Southern Europe, and especially from Italy. This is most marked in relation to the crime of homicide" (US Immigration Commission 1911, 2). Southern Europeans were one of the groups targeted by the Johnson-Reed Act in 1924, and the Dillingham Commission findings provided some of the justification for the deliberate limiting of Italian immigrants through the imposition of national quotas. The Irish, whom restrictionists also wanted to limit through national quotas, were also found to commit offenses against public policy more often than other national groups However, the report notes that the increase in these crimes could also have resulted from the growth of cities and the increase in forbidden acts because of this growth more than from immigration itself.

The Dillingham Commission report seemed to verify the longstanding beliefs in immigrant criminality that would later be used as a justification for national quotas under the Johnson-Reed. Oddly, it was unconcerned with Mexican immigrants even though among the "racial" groups examined, Mexican nationals came in sixth in the total number of prisoners in the United States as of 1908 and were second to Italians in the total number of individuals detained for murder and attempted murder in both 1904 and 1908 (US Immigration Commission 1911). Why, then, did the report dedicate so little time to discussing the dangers of Mexican immigration, while focusing so much on the crime rates among European nationals? This was likely owing to the fact that the commission was motivated by a desire to reduce immigration from "undesirable" European countries, while Mexican immigration remained a secondary concern. This would of course not be the case after passage of the Johnson-Reed Act, but the US attitude toward Mexican immigration during this period can best be described as "complicated."

The Dillingham Commission report provided the justification for national quotas that would be established under the Johnson-Reed Act by painting southern and eastern European immigrants as a criminal threat to the nation. This criminality was not linked to the external circumstances faced by the Irish, the Italians, and other vilified European immigrant groups, but instead to something inherent to their ethnicity. Reducing the immigration of these national groups was a means of controlling them, of limiting the threat they posed to the nation because of their propensity for crime. Of course, ethnicity in no way predisposes someone to criminality, but constructing them as in some way of lower moral stock preserved the racial and ethnic hierarchies of the United States. It gave those who had come in earlier immigrant waves and were native born a special status and superiority, while conferring a lower status on those immigrants who were less white because of their ethnicity. This criminality ascribed to earlier waves of immigrants would inextricably become linked to the illegality of Mexican immigrants in the period following Johnson-Reed. Criminality and illegality were deliberate political constructions to justify the control of populations believed to be different or racially inferior. Unlike past immigrant groups, undocumented immigrants would be stereotyped as criminals, and they would be treated as no immigrant group before them had been treated.

Mexican Immigration, Criminality, and the Evolution of Immigration Policy, 1848–1929

The Dillingham Commission may have ignored Mexican immigration in its discussions for two reasons. On the one hand, nativism in the first quarter of the twentieth century was largely directed at European immigrants, who were seen as being of a lesser form of whiteness (Higham 1994; M. F. Jacobson 1998). On the other hand, Mexican immigration was both necessary and valuable for the development of the Southwest. Despite Mexicans being the "iconic illegal aliens," Mexican immigration to the United States had a long history and would not even be regulated until the 1920s, with very little attention paid to the "Mexican problem" until undesirable European immigration was significantly reduced through national quotas (Ngai 2004).

After the Mexican-American War (1846–48), Mexico ceded what is now the Southwest to the United States, and former Mexican nationals who did not want to relocate to Mexican territory were allowed to naturalize as US citizens (Ngai 2004). Even though whiteness was prerequisite for naturalization, Latinos could gain citizenship following the Mexican-American War because they were technically Caucasian. No restrictions were placed on Mexican immigration, and Mexican labor played a large role in the development of the Southwest (Hernandez 2010; Tichenor 2002). By the 1920s the Southwest had become one of the nation's most valuable agricultural regions, with approximately 31 million acres of crops, requiring a large work force (Hernandez 2010, 23). At the same time, the access of southwestern agribusiness to other sources of labor during the late nineteenth and early twentieth centuries was cut off. Chinese, Japanese, and other labor from Asia was restricted through the Chinese Exclusion Act (1882), the Gentleman's Agreement between the United States and Japan (1907), and the Asiatic Barred Zone (1917), respectively. This meant that by the 1920s Mexicans accounted for much of the work force in the Southwest (Hernandez 2010; Ngai 2004). Mexican laborers regularly crossed back and forth between the two countries to work while restrictionists, focusing their energies on European immigration, for the most part ignored them.

There was little change in the first decade of the twentieth century. Mexican laborers continued to move freely across the border, while attempts to restrict European immigration largely failed to find support in Congress between 1900 and 1910. Mexican immigration during this time received little, if any, attention from federal lawmakers. The unrestricted crossing of Mexican immigrants was not seen as a criminal act even if after passage of the Immigration Act of 1917 it was technically an administrative violation to cross into the United States anywhere other than at a designated border crossing (Ngai 2004). Even immigration inspectors ignored Mexican laborers entering the United States to work, and the Immigration Bureau did not even consider Mexican immigration to be within its purview, instead seeing it as regulated by labor demands in border states (Ngai 2004, 64). Mexicans were regarded as a valuable source of labor not only because of their proximity but also because they were seen as less threatening than other foreign workers (Kanstroom 2007, 156). An article from the *New York Times* in 1920 nicely sums up the view of Mexican immigrants during the period, quoting Vernon Mc-Combs, a superintendent of the United-Methodist Latin America Missions in southern California as stating, "They hold fine possibilities of citizenship, being sturdy, independent and filled with racial pride. To the best of my belief, there isn't a Mexican tramp in the United States. But despite their good qualities, they are, we must remember, illiterate and grossly misinformed about the United States" (Breitigam 1920). Perceptions of Mexican immigrants reflected a good deal of racial paternalism, but there were few perceptions of threat, at least while Mexican labor remained a necessity and Mexican laborers were found more appealing than laborers from southern or eastern European countries, who were seen not only as being of inferior stock but also as potential political agitators and troublemakers (Tichenor 2002).

In 1917 the first significant immigration act of the twentieth century was passed, requiring all immigrants to pay a head tax and to submit to a literacy test. Both requirements were targeted at immigrants from southern and eastern Europe (M. F. Jacobson 1998). Initially, Mexican immigrants also were subject to both the head tax and the literacy test, but during World War I they were exempted from both to facilitate US access to Mexican labor (Tichenor 2002, 142). Mexican laborers poured into the Southwest during this time, and even bars on contract labor were eased (Kanstroom 2007, 156). After the war these exemptions were removed, and Mexicans were required to apply for US admission at a valid point of entry, though there was still little regulation of the southern border, which remained unpatrolled until the formation of the Border Patrol in 1924 (Ngai 2004, 64).

The formation of the Border Patrol and the passage of the Johnson-Reed Act of 1924 represented an important victory for restrictionists in

Congress, who had long argued for greater regulation of immigration, as well as more concrete ways to reduce the flow of immigration from southern and eastern Europe. The Johnson-Reed Act set quotas for immigration at 2 percent of the total number of individuals of a given nationality residing in the United States as recorded on the 1890 Census, though the Western Hemisphere was exempt from these quotas. This significantly reduced immigration from the "undesirable" countries of Europe, while favoring immigrants from northern and western Europe. The Johnson-Reed Act resulted more broadly in a drop in immigration as the result of the quotas it introduced, with European immigration being reduced from 364,339 in 1924 to 148,366 in 1925 (Ngai 2004).

During the 1920s, nativist calls to restrict Mexican immigration also began to grow despite the lack of quotas, with a spike in scholarly articles on the subject of the "Mexican Problem" from nineteen between 1910 and 1920 to fifty-one between 1920 and 1930 (Nevins 2010, 105). In the past, Mexican immigration had avoided the quota for a few reasons. First, because of the value of Mexican labor to American industry, many Republicans and Southern Democrats opposed any serious restriction of Mexican immigration. In addition, business interests in the southwestern United States lobbied hard to preserve access to Mexican labor, often testifying before Senate and House committees on the necessity of Mexican labor (Hernandez 2010; Tichenor 2002). A desire for friendly relations with Mexico also played a role, as the imposition of quotas was seen as a potential refutation of notions of pan-Americanism (Tichenor 2002). Finally, it was impossible to patrol the entirety of the US-Mexico border, particularly with a relatively small and undertrained Border Patrol, which would make any quota difficult to enforce. Nevertheless, there were calls to restrict Mexican immigration during the floor debate on the Johnson-Reed Act, which presaged the later problematizing of undocumented immigration as a criminal violation and marked the beginning of a new period in its history. The formation of the Border Patrol and the passage of Johnson-Reed also marked the beginning of increased hostility to Mexican immigration and the use of administrative actions to attempt to reduce it, which would culminate in the passage of S. 5094 and Mexican Repatriation in 1929 (Ngai 2004).

The Johnson-Reed Act and the End of Unrestricted Immigration

The twentieth century would see a concerted push to limit immigration into the United States, particularly from countries in southern and eastern Europe, whose immigrants were seen as a lesser form of whiteness and both a cultural and an economic threat to American citizens. While Chinese immigration had been all but eliminated by the Chinese Exclusion Act in 1882, European immigration, particularly from southern and eastern Europe, had boomed. Immigration from countries like Greece, Italy, Russia, and Hungary made up a large percentage of the roughly six million immigrants who would arrive in the United States between 1901 and 1910 (Tichenor 2002, 115). Groups like the Immigration Restriction League (IRL) feared the economic and cultural impact these immigrants might have on the United States and advocated policies to reduce immigration overall, but particularly from these "undesirable" countries. The IRL characterized southern and eastern Europeans as being racially inferior and pushed for the implementation of a literacy test to reduce the flow of immigration from these areas (Tichenor 2002).

The forty-two-volume report by the Dillingham Commission, released in 1911, seemed to support many of the stereotypes of southern and eastern Europeans held by groups like the IRL. The commission's study, the largest of immigration in the United States at the time, involved three years of research by a staff of three hundred with a budget of $1 million (Tichenor 2002). The commission's report seemed to validate many of the concerns of restrictionists. New immigrants were found to be less skilled, less assimilated, and more prone to criminal behavior, with Italians being singled out as more likely to commit crimes of violence. The commission's report covered all three threat frames—the economic threat posed to American labor by a large, unskilled work force who would be willing to work for less and under worse conditions; the cultural threat posed by immigrants who were not assimilated as fully as past generations and perhaps never would be; and the criminal threat posed by ethnic groups who seemed more disposed to violent crime than their predecessors from other countries (US Commission on Immigration 1911). The Dillingham Commission report was a victory for restrictionists, who now could base their arguments for limiting immigration from southern and eastern Europe on hard numbers rather than anecdotes.

The Dillingham Commission also gave restrictionists what they wanted in terms of policy prescriptions, recommending a literacy test, an increased head tax, and limiting immigration based on a quota system. The IRL saw the report as a major victory, so much so that their lobbyist, James Patten, ordered ten thousand copies of the report and another twenty thousand of its summary (Tichenor 2002, 131). Groups like the IRL pushed hard for the enactment of the literacy test as a requirement for immigration in the belief that it would seriously limit undesirable immigration from southern and eastern European countries. They succeeded in 1917 with the passage of the Immigration Act of 1917, which included not only a literacy test but also an Asiatic barred zone and an increased head tax.

The victory was short-lived, though, as the IRL quickly realized that the literacy test was not having its intended effect because many immigrants from southern and eastern Europe could pass it (Tichenor 2002). This led restrictionists to seek a new way to reduce what they saw as undesirable immigration, and in 1921 a plan submitted by William Dillingham following the committee's report was resurrected (Tichenor 2002). Dillingham had suggested a quota system, which had been largely ignored in favor of the literacy test. On the heels of World War I a spike in immigration and the Red Scare that accompanied the Bolshevik Revolution in Russia led to a revival of quotas as a potential solution (Tichenor 2002).

In 1921 the Quota Law was passed as an emergency measure to choke off immigration. The law put in place temporary quotas that capped immigration at 3 percent of the foreign-born population in the United States as of 1910. It limited immigration overall to 350,000, for the first time in US history strictly limiting the number of immigrants who could enter, though a number of exemptions were created. Those who had resided for one year in a country in the Western Hemisphere, those whose immigration was regulated by treaty, and a number of different employment classes were not counted in the quotas, which in practice meant that far more immigrants were being admitted than was suggested (Foster Global 2007). The Quota Law was twice renewed by Congress, but many believed something more permanent was needed to ensure that immigration restriction would endure.

The Johnson-Reed Act of 1924 was one of the most important pieces of immigration legislation in US history. It introduced permanent quotas for immigration that would continue through 1952 and greatly influenced the cultural contours of America through national-origins quotas. As stated above, these were set at 2 percent of the total population of each national group in the United States in 1890, which limited southern and eastern Europeans, while privileging those from northern and western Europe. The Johnson-Reed Act also reduced total immigration even further by setting the overall limit at 164,667, which represented 2 percent of the number of foreign born in the United States in 1890 and was a significant drop from the 350,000 allowed under the Quota

Law (Immigration Act of May 26th, 1924). It was a breakthrough for those immigration restrictionists who had unsuccessfully tried to limit immigration through the introduction of a literacy test. This discriminatory desire to privilege northern and western Europe while limiting those from southern and eastern Europe was noted by Senator LeBaron Colt of Rhode Island: "If you go back to 1890, you have 87 percent from northern and western Europe and 13 percent from southern and eastern Europe. Do you wonder that the 6,000,000 people from southern and eastern Europe claim that this is a gross discrimination against them?" (65th Cong. Rec., 5413).

After World War I there were also concerns about "hyphenated Americans," those who maintained and celebrated their ethnic heritage, and a push for more aggressive Americanization programs. Some states adopted legislation that denied employment to the foreign born who did not intend to pursue citizenship; Iowa even went so far as to outlaw speaking languages other than English (Tichenor 2002, 140). Presidents Theodore Roosevelt and Woodrow Wilson were proponents of the Americanization of the foreign born, and the concern regarding assimilation helped drive the passage of the literacy test in 1917 because national conformity was easier if there was greater cultural homogeneity in the United States itself (Tichenor 2002). This was reflected in the comments of Senator William Harris of Georgia, who expressed grave reservations regarding the Americanization of foreign-born whites and their children. In a lengthy tirade, Senator Harris argued that "the Americanization of these thirty-six and a third million of our population is, in many cases, only skin deep and is merely a mask to be quickly thrown aside when the interests of their fatherland are involved. . . . There is a grave danger to our country from immigrants who live in their own groups, read papers in their own language, work, live and vote in their own groups, and not as Americans" (65th Cong. Rec., 5738). The concerns regarding assimilation, particularly of those groups who were seen as inferior, played a large role in the Johnson-Reed debate, with Senator Harris pushing for an even stricter restriction based on a 1 percent quota or even a temporary ban on immigration (65th Cong. Rec., 5738).

While the Johnson-Reed Act divided Europeans into discrete nationalities for the purposes of quotas, it excluded anyone who was ineligible for citizenship (Ngai 1999). This exclusion was meant to either significantly reduce or eliminate immigration from Asia, particularly China and Japan, as nationals from Asian countries were not eligible for naturalization. While immigration from China had been addressed by the earlier Chinese Exclusion Act, loopholes permitted some Chinese immigration, which continued to be a cause of concern, though this was secondary to concerns over immigration from Japan. Japanese immigration had been reduced by the Gentleman's Agreement of 1907, which allowed for the immigration of the wives and children of Japanese citizens already in the United States, while Japan agreed to deny visas to any laborers hoping to work in America (Ngai 2004; Tichenor 2002). On the part of Japan, this agreement was signed to prevent the kind of restriction seen under the Chinese Exclusion Act. For the United States, this was a way of limiting Japanese immigration, while avoiding any slight to the Japanese government. Japan was both respected and seen as a friend at the time of congressional debate over Johnson-Reed, as is reflected by the comments of Republican senator Samuel Shortridge of California, who in pushing for Japanese immigration to be included in Johnson-Reed was careful to note that "toward Japan this nation meditates no harm. We are not conspiring against the nation. . . . We do not hate her. . . . We would have the most cordial relations with her—international relations, trade relations" (65th Cong. Rec., 5747). Many were quick to point out that the Japanese government itself limited immigration from other Asian countries like China and Korea, so that the United States was not doing anything the Japanese government was not doing (65th Cong. Rec., 5809).

The Gentleman's Agreement was a subject of concern and suspicion because it was not an act of Congress, nor could many members even explain it. In the debate over Johnson-Reed, Senator Claude Swanson of Virginia noted, "I have never seen anybody yet who could define to me what the gentlemen's agreement is about which we hear so much. It seems to me it is as indefinite as vapor" (65th Cong. Rec., 5828). While the primary goal of Johnson-Reed may have been to restrict southern and eastern European immigration, it also sought to reduce or eliminate Asian immigration and establish congressional control over Japanese immigration. Japan, China, and India would receive the minimum quota of 100 under Johnson-Reed, but these individuals could not actually be Japanese, Chinese, or Indian, since they would be ineligible for citizenship, and thus immigration, if they were (Ngai 1999). The Johnson-Reed Act would severely limit immigration from Asian countries for more than twenty-five years, until June 27, 1952, when the McCarran-Walter Act removed all racial restrictions for naturalization (Ngai 2004; Tichenor 2002).

Overall, criminality was a lesser concern in the debate over Johnson-

Reed than was either assimilation (cultural threat) or employment (economic threat). Immigrants from southern and eastern Europe were portrayed as being a threat to the American worker and to the country's cultural identity, but they were less often painted as criminals, possibly owing to the groups Johnson-Reed sought to limit. As mentioned earlier, Japan was seen as a friend despite the desire to curb the immigration of Japanese nationals, and while southern and eastern European immigration was demonized in the debate, the number of nationalities regional identifier encompassed made criminality more difficult to attribute to the group as a whole. The Dillingham Commission may have found evidence of greater criminality among Italian immigrants, but they did not find the same evidence for Polish immigrants, for example, which limited how broadly the criminality narrative could be applied.

Mexican Immigrants and the Johnson-Reed Act

Johnson-Reed marked a turning point in US immigration policy, the beginning of a shift of attention away from European immigration to Mexican immigration for the first time. One way of determining the relative importance of Mexican immigration in the debate around Johnson-Reed is to examine the frequency with which the term *Mexican* came up compared with the names of other nationalities in House and Senate remarks on the bill. Table 1.1 shows the top ten national, regional, or racial groups mentioned in Senate and House remarks on Johnson-Reed. I counted instances in which the speakers were referring to immigrants themselves rather than their countries of origin. I ran the congressional debate on Johnson-Reed through a word-search function, which provided frequencies for each nationality. To ensure the accuracy of the electronic count, nationalities were selected randomly, and a manual word count was performed as well, with no significant inconsistencies found between the two.

Table 1.1 reveals that Japanese immigration was the primary concern of Senate members in the debate over Johnson-Reed, but this was followed by Mexican immigration at a distant second. Mexican immigration was mentioned 107 times during Senate debate, which would seem to indicate that Mexican immigration was of great concern to the Senate, at least in regard to immigration policy. It is not surprising that Japanese immigration came up much more frequently, as Mexican immigration was believed to be less of a problem than Asian immigration at the time. Most Asian national groups had been barred from immigrating to the United States through congressional legislation like the Chinese Exclu-

TABLE 1.1. Mentions of national, regional, and racial identifiers in the Johnson-Reed debate

IDENTIFIER	SENATE	HOUSE
Japanese	525	382
Mexican	107	150
European	81	145
Chinese	80	136
British/English	39	121
German	36	116
Canadian	36	109
Italian	35	93
Negro	27	83
Russian	20	64

sion Act and the Asiatic Barred Zone, which was part of the Immigration Act of 1917, but immigration from Japan was subject to the Gentleman's Agreement of 1907.

As mentioned earlier, the Gentleman's Agreement was viewed with suspicion by members of the Senate, with many members of Congress citing the lack of transparency in the Gentleman's Agreement as a reason for applying quotas to Japan. Senator Shortridge noted that "it is very difficult, indeed, to determine how many come under the treaty and how many have come under this so-called 'gentleman's agreement.' Nor is it easy to ascertain how many have smuggled themselves in by all sorts of subterfuges, on board ship or across the border" (65th Cong. Rec., 5804). One of the main concerns senators expressed in regard to Japanese immigration was the potential threat it posed to American labor, particularly in California. Senator Shortridge connected the prior concerns about Chinese laborers in California, which had led to the Chinese Exclusion Act, to Japanese immigration by citing the difficulty Americans had in competing with "oriental" labor. Speaking without the aid of a prepared text, Shortridge stated, "I say we are opposed to oriental immigration because the American father, mother, child, with our type and standard of life and living, can not successfully compete with them. . . . Is there anyone who wishes us to engage in that impossible competition?" (65th Cong. Rec., 5743). There were also concerns with the foreignness of Japanese culture. Kenneth McKellar, of Tennessee, managed to praise the Japanese while also painting them as a cultural threat: "I have no unkindly feeling for Japan; Japan is a great nation, but her people are wholly different from ours. Different in color, different in language, different in thought and aspiration. They can not and they do not assimilate with us" (65th Cong. Rec., 5957). The Japanese were rarely painted as a lower form of civilization; instead the focus was on how Japanese individuals fundamentally differed from Americans. In a similar vein to comments made by Senator McKellar, the comments on the Japanese made by Democrat William Bruce of Maryland were emblematic of this perceived difference and more specific than those of the senator from Tennessee: "They cherish different religious faiths from ours; their traditions, their customs, their habits of thought and feeling, their economic wants and standards are all utterly unlike ours" (65th Cong. Rec., 6312). Throughout the Senate debate on Johnson-Reed these same concerns were raised time and again as a reason to include Japan in the bill despite the relatively small number of Japanese immigrants who had come to the United States in 1923, which was estimated during the debate to be to only be 399 persons when immigration and emigration were both considered (65th Cong. Rec., 5744).

The large number of mentions of Japanese immigrants in Senate debate was largely the result of, first, dissatisfaction with the method being used to limit immigration from Japan and a general suspicion of and dissatisfaction with the Gentlemen's Agreement, and second, the perceived cultural threat from Japanese immigration. Concerns about race mixing, the "foreign" culture of the Japanese, and the economic threat they posed, particularly in Pacific states like California, were cited as reasons for subjecting the Japanese to the racial quotas of Johnson-Reed. Just the application of quotas to Japan based on the 1890 Census would have reduced immigration greatly. When asked to estimate the number of Japanese immigrants who could legally enter the United States based on 2 percent of the 1890 Census, Senator Colt responded that it would be at most be a few hundred (65th Cong. Rec., 5417). While thousands of Japanese immigrants had entered the United States in 1923, an almost equal number had left, resulting in a net gain of fewer than four hundred individuals (65th Cong. Rec., 5744). This begs the question why Japan was such a focus in the debate, though the answer appears to be a simple one: while there supposedly had been a net gain of only a few hundred, there could have been more. Since the Gentlemen's Agreement imposed no limits on Japanese immigration, there were no guarantees that the net gain would always be as low as it had been in 1923.

There were also discussions of applying the quotas under Johnson-Reed to Mexican immigration, but there was resistance to this. On the side of restriction, the economic threat of Mexican immigrants was frequently cited. A few concerns were raised in reference to trying to apply quotas to Mexico, with one being simply the inability of the Border Patrol to actually stop undocumented immigration across its nearly two-thousand-mile length. "Just imagine what the result will be if we pass this law," stated Republican senator David Reed of Pennsylvania—the Reed in Johnson-Reed. "Obviously, we are not going to pass it unless we mean in good faith to enforce it. Imagine trying to patrol thousands of miles of uninhabited country along that river, which can be waded along much of its length, with brush so dense that an officer cannot see a man more than 10 feet off, and imagine to yourselves what it will cost us to enforce that border patrol to keep out these 62,000 Mexicans" (65th Cong. Rec., 6624). The Border Patrol was still in its infancy, with only a small and relatively untrained force at its disposal (Hernandez 2010; Ngai 2004). Even had there been more men available, it is very unlikely that they could have fully secured anything close to a significant percentage of the border. In addition, there was a longstanding tradition of unfettered crossing between Mexico and the United States for the purposes of labor. This norm created a major obstacle to border security: both immigrants and employers wanted to continue this relationship, and immigration officials were ambivalent, regardless of whether free movement of people was now prohibited (Ngai 2004).

The inclusion of Mexican immigration in Johnson-Reed faced a further hurdle because of concerns that the quota would endanger the bill not only because of resistance from industries reliant on Mexican labor but also owing to the difficulties inherent in limiting immigration from Mexico. During the House debate, this was expressed by Democrat Cyrenus Cole, who, citing fellow Democrat John Box of Texas stated, "The same gentleman confessed, or admitted, that the committee found the task so great that they did not dare to extend the restrictions to Canada and to Mexico, in fear of losing support for the bill" (65th Cong. Rec., 6476). So while there were concerns regarding Mexican immigration, there was no dedicated push for restriction. This differed from the attitude toward Japanese immigration, which many wanted to see restricted owing to cultural and economic fears but also in large part owing to concerns over the Gentleman's Agreement and which was easier to restrict because an ocean separated Japan from the United States.

The Framing of Immigration during the Johnson-Reed Debate

One way of examining how Mexicans were characterized compared with other immigrant groups is to break down the positive and negative attributes assigned to a particular group in the debate over Johnson-Reed to a set of *frames*. As discussed in the introduction, three threat frames are typically referenced regarding immigration in the United States. The economic threat frame portrays immigrants as a danger to the American worker, either because they take jobs that should go to the native born or because they drive down wages. Immigrants may also be characterized as a burden on social services and thus the taxpayer. The cultural threat frame focuses on issues of assimilation and the undermining of American identity by foreigners with inferior traditions. Lastly, immigrants can be painted as a criminal threat, as being inclined to violence or criminality, as a way of justifying exclusion. It is this latter frame that is the focus of this book and of the analysis of the Johnson-Reed debate, but it is useful to compare the three frames to determine what the dominant frame was during the Johnson-Reed debate, as well as during the debates over S. 5094, IRCA, and IIRIRA.

To code these frames, a number of words or phrases were isolated and classified as representing either a positive or a negative economic frame on the basis of whether the immigrants were portrayed as economic contributors or an economic burden; a positive or a negative cultural frame based on the positive or negative attributes they were assigned on the basis of their ethnicity or national origin; and a positive or negative criminality frame on the basis of whether the immigrants in question were portrayed as more or less inclined to criminality or associated with crime (table 1.2).

In coding the debate, I chose to code frames on the basis of individual remarks by members of Congress rather than to code multiple mentions of the same frame in each comment. My intention was to examine the commonality of these frames, while not allowing multiple mentions of a frame in a single comment to exaggerate how dominant it was. For example, if a member of Congress mentioned an economic threat from Japanese immigration seven times during one comment in the debate, only one point was assigned. However, if the senator brought up this same concern later in the debate, another point was added to the economic threat cell. Multiple independent frames could be coded for in each comment, so if a senator mentioned both a negative economic

TABLE 1.2. Positive or negative frame coding

ECONOMIC		CULTURAL		CRIMINAL	
POSITIVE	NEGATIVE	POSITIVE	NEGATIVE	POSITIVE	NEGATIVE
Improve economy	Take jobs	Contribute to culture	Don't assimilate	Law-abiding	Stealing/theft
Labor demands	Burden on services	Assimilate	Racial threat	Follow rules	Smuggling
Hard workers	Don't pay taxes	Shared values	Different values	Obey laws	Fraud
	Work too hard	Family-oriented	Undesirable	Honest	Violence
	Hurt unions		Illiterate		Crime
	Lower wages		Uneducated		Criminals
					Drugs
					Gangs

TABLE 1.3. Threat frames in the Senate Johnson-Reed debate: Unique mentions / number of senators mentioning, by immigrant group

FRAME	JAPANESE	MEXICAN	ITALIAN
Positive economic	0/0	8/6	0/0
Negative economic	4/3	6/4	0/0
Positive cultural	7/5	6/4	3/3
Negative cultural	14/9	9/5	0/0
Positive criminal	0/0	1/1	0/0
Negative criminal	5/2	4/4	2/1

frame and a negative cultural frame in the same comment, both were tallied. This was done to highlight the number of unique mentions, since some senators made long speeches about immigrant groups that hit on the same threat trope repeatedly. Unique mentions are more representative of the norm of the immigration debate and don't allow one member of Congress to bias the data. Table 1.3 also notes the number of senators who mentioned that particular threat or attribute.

Table 1.3 reveals some interesting trends. First, a number of senators praised the economic contribution made by Mexican immigrants to the United States, with this being mentioned eight times by six different senators during the debate over Johnson-Reed. These contributions were balanced by four senators who saw Mexican labor as a threat to American workers, with many pointing out that without border control there was the potential for an oversupply of Mexican labor, which would potentially hurt US labor. John Shields, of Tennessee, pointed out that under Johnson-Reed "from 200,000 to 225,000 Canadians and Mexicans will come annually to this country, largely men that engage in agriculture, and especially the Mexicans." Speaking of American workers, he continued, "I believe they ought to be well-paid and I do not believe they ought to have any cheap competition or low standards of living such as this foreign labor brings to them" (65th Cong. Rec., 6610).

The economic threat frame was challenged for dominance in the debate by the nine mentions of the cultural inferiority and inassimilable nature of Mexican immigrants by five senators. Four senators argued that Mexican, particularly Spanish, culture posed no threat to US culture and that Mexicans made fine additions to the country. Democratic senator Alva Adams of Colorado commented that "he [the Mexican] is not a bad citizen. He is not an anarchist. He is not lawless. As a matter of fact, the Spanish speaking people and those of Spanish descent are good citizens in our community, and they are citizens much needed" (65th Cong. Rec., 6625). However, Senator Frank Willis, a Republican from Ohio who pushed for national quotas to be applied to Mexico, argued that Mexicans were, "unfortunately, practically without education, and largely without experience in self-government, and in most cases not at all qualified for present citizenship or for assimilation into this country" (65th Cong. Rec., 6631). One of the most incendiary comments drawing on the cultural threat frame was made by Matthew Neely, of West Virginia, who proclaimed,

> On the basis of merit Mexico is the last country in the world to which we should grant special favor or extend a peculiar privilege. She has committed more offenses against the American Government, outraged more American citizens, and usurped more American property rights than any other nation in the world. . . . It is high time for us to realize that this is our country, and that it is our duty to defend it against all enemies. It is our duty to defend it not only against enemies in arms but against the millions of physically, mentally, and morally inferior men and women scattered over Europe, Asia, Africa, Mexico, and the islands of the sea, who, as prospective immigrants, are awaiting their opportunity to rush to our shores. (65th Cong. Rec, 6625)

It must be acknowledged that in general the debate did not ascribe negative cultural traits specifically to Mexicans but instead questioned why undesirable European countries were subject to the quota, while Mexico was not, as in both cases the United States was receiving immigrants of a lower quality than the native stock. This is highlighted by the latter part of the comment from Senator Neely, which lumps Mexican immigration together with European, African, and Asian immigration in its undesirability.

The criminal threat frame, usually based on undocumented crossing or a perception that the foreign born were more inclined to crime, took third in both the number of unique mentions and the number of senators who mentioned it. Senator Neely, in pushing for the inclusion of Mexicans in Johnson-Reed, posited that "the all-compelling reason we should for the present prohibit or at least most rigidly restrict immigration, including that from Mexico, is discovered in the fact that our foreign-born population is largely responsible for the lawlessness, the violence, and the crime that are burdening our taxpayers, blackening our record, overcrowding our jails and penitentiaries, disgracing our Nation, and jeopardizing the safety of all law-abiding citizens" (65th Cong. Rec, 6626). Many of the comments regarding the criminality of Mexican immigrants—the majority of the comments that were coded as referencing the criminal threat frame—had to do with their undocumented entry, which circumvented both the literacy test and the head tax. They were only coded as referencing this frame when specific words suggesting criminality, such as *surreptitiously* or *illegally,* were used in discussing Mexican immigration into the United States. *Illegal immigrant* or *illegal alien* had not yet become the common name for undocumented immigration and was instead often used to describe the method of entry.

The criminality frame was applied not only to Mexican immigrants but also more generally to the border itself, with multiple mentions of the use of the Mexican border as an illegal crossing point for Europeans and Asians who otherwise could not legally enter the country. While these mentions were not included in the coding of the criminality frame, they are worth discussing, since this extension of the frame to both the immigrants and the border itself continues today, with discussions of terrorists potentially crossing the Mexican border with the intention of carrying out attacks against the United States. This extension of the frame was reflected in the Johnson-Reed debate, particularly in a comment by Senator Willis in which he quoted the immigration inspector at San Antonio as saying about those crossing the southern border that "these aliens for the most part are inadmissible to this country and highly undesirable as residents. Among them are anarchists, criminals and radicals who have been unable to secure visas from American consuls in Europe to enable them to secure steamship passage" (65th Cong. Rec., 6621). Concerns about the criminality of immigrants from Mexico were thus not necessarily directed only at Mexicans but also at those of other nationalities who it was feared could exploit the lack of security on the southern border, something that has been echoed in modern times by concerns that al-Qaeda or the Islamic State could exploit the porousness of the border to gain entry to the United States to commit acts of terrorism.

These comments were largely reflective of the Senate debate on Mexican immigration during Johnson-Reed, which tended to be about the need for Mexican labor and the impact Mexican culture would have on the United States. The criminal threat frame was not relied upon as heavily as were arguments about the threat posed to American workers by Mexican immigrants or the difficulties in assimilating this group. The notion of immigrant criminality would be raised much more often in the debate over S. 5094 in 1929, in which Mexican immigration was the sole focus. At the time of Johnson-Reed, Mexican immigration was far from a first concern, with both European and Asian immigration seen as more problematic and more pressing issues.

The characterization of Mexicans differed in many ways from the characterization of the Japanese in the debate over Johnson-Reed. While the Japanese were frequently praised for their culture, they were also characterized as unassimilable, as an economic threat, and as agents of a foreign power. During Senate debate on Johnson-Reed the Japanese were not mentioned as anything but an economic threat to Americans, whereas Mexicans were seen as economically necessary. This difference was owing in part to how both immigrant groups were perceived. Japanese culture, while seen as alien, was praised for all its admirable characteristics, while Mexican culture was rarely constructed as either as foreign or as dangerous as Japanese culture. Addressing the desire on the part of US labor groups to see Japanese immigration reduced or cut off entirely, Senator Shortridge argued, "All appreciate what I am poorly stating, namely, that inasmuch as these people can never become citizens, inasmuch as they are alien in tongue, in instincts, in habits, in mode of life, are ineligible to citizenship, it is undesirable that they enter this country to abide en masse in any State of the Union" (65th Cong. Rec., 5745). Shortridge also decried the coming "Japanization" of California, citing Hawaii as an example of cultural changes resulting from Japanese immigration and high birth rates (65th Cong. Rec., 5804). While this cultural threat framing of Japanese immigration was common, many also praised Japan as a nation and the Japanese as a people. In discussing quotas for Japan, Claude Swanson of Virginia stated, "I have great respect for Japan as a nation and its people have many admirable qualities." (65th Cong. Rec., 6302). Many senators expressed admiration for Japan as a nation, if not for the Japanese people and their culture.

Mexican immigration was portrayed in terms of illegality and criminality more often than was Japanese immigration. Of the five mentions of Japanese criminality in the Johnson-Reed debate, all but one were made by Senator Shortridge. On the other hand, Mexican criminality was mentioned by three different senators and one House member during the Johnson-Reed Senate debate: Senators Reed, Shields, and Willis and Representative Cole all touched on the criminality trait in discussions of Mexican immigration.

A statement that Senator Willis requested be inserted into the Congressional Record, dealing with the smuggling of immigrants across the border by Mexican "coyotes," is illustrative. Willis quoted the immigration inspector in charge of the San Antonio district as saying of the coyote, "The Mexican border smuggler is an extremely dangerous person to deal with. He goes 'armed to the teeth' and does not hesitate to fire upon officers at sight. A number of Federal and State officers have been killed on this border in the recent past by these smugglers, and it has been more luck than anything else that many of our men have not been killed. There is hardly a week goes by that they are not fired upon" (65th Cong. Rec., 6622). In portrayals of the Japanese as criminals, they were typically characterized as one of the groups being smuggled into the country by Mexican coyotes. Violence was absent from the negative characterizations of the Japanese, while Mexicans were portrayed not just as illegal entrants but as being responsible for the smuggling of both Asians and Europeans into US border states. For instance, Senator Shortridge said of the Japanese that "it is impossible to state accurately how many have been smuggled in, because they come in surreptitiously" (65th Cong. Rec., 5746). Japanese immigrants were considered criminals because they entered the country "surreptitiously," but Mexicans were portrayed as both illegal and dangerous.

What is surprising is how little mention there was of European national groups in the Johnson-Reed debate. Europeans were the primary target of national-origin quotas, and yet Italians, whom the 1911 Dillingham Commission had found more likely to commit crimes of personal violence, ranked eighth in overall mentions in the Senate, which was dominated by discussions of Asian immigration, which Johnson-Reed would have little hand in outside of creating a pan-ethnic Asian category for the purposes of quotas. This category was likely created because some members of Congress wanted to include Mexico or Japan in the quota system, while Italians, Poles, and Irish would already be restricted under the national quota system, since it would draw on the 1890 Census, thus permitting far fewer immigrants from these countries to enter.

Johnson-Reed in the House

The emphasis in the House debate was similar, at least with respect to the attention paid to Japanese immigration, but there were also some important differences (see table 1.1). In the House, Mexicans were only in the top ten for mentioned nationalities, coming in seventh overall in total individual mentions, while European and Italian immigration received far more mentions, as was expected for a bill that was tailored to limit undesirable European immigration. Asian immigration was the top concern of House debate, with 382 mentions of Japanese immigrants, compared with 150 mentions of Europeans and 115 of Italians. Mexican immigrants were mentioned 109 times over the course of House debate on Johnson-Reed. In many cases, this was by representatives who wanted to extend national quotas to Mexico and Canada, with an emphasis on the importance of these quotas for restricting the immigration of Mexican nationals. Indeed, in much of the debate on extending the quotas to Mexico it was argued that if Europeans were to be excluded, Mexicans should be as well, particularly as they were even less desirable than the least desirable European. Republican representative Martin Madden of Illinois pointed out that

> this bill is reported by the rigid immigration restrictionists, and yet the bill leaves open the doors for perhaps the worst element that comes into the United States—the Mexican peon. He comes in without restriction, without regulation, without any attempted opposition. He comes in, and he does not go back. He gets into all the southwestern section of the United States and the western section and he supplies these sections with such labor as they need—Oregon, Idaho, California, Washington, Texas, and the border States, like Arizona and New Mexico. They bring them in and employ them everywhere, and yet you refuse to let White men into other ports. The West and the Southwest take care of themselves. (65th Cong. Rec., 5887)

Madden's mention of the West and the Southwest in the final sentence is indicative of the divisions between those in border states, who in many cases depended on Mexican labor, and those outside those states, who saw the admission of Mexicans as a threat. Much of the criticism of Mexicans in the debate over Johnson-Reed came from those who did not benefit from having Mexican workers.

Later in the debate, Patrick O'Sullivan, a Democratic representative from Connecticut, made the same argument, not only stating that Mexican immigration needed to be restricted but making an explicit comparison between the groups that would be restricted under Johnson-Reed and Mexican immigrants. "I do not know what standard is used to measure desirability," said O'Sullivan, "but I do know that the average Italian is as much superior to the average Mexican as a full-blooded Airedale is to a mongrel. Yet this bill will permit every Mexican in Mexico to enter the United States, and the same bill limits the number of Italians to 3,912 immigrants" (65th Cong. Rec., 5900). The lack of limits on Mexican immigration was obviously a concern to some, yet Mexican immigration still received less attention than did Asian or European immigration during the House debate.

One possible reason for this relative lack of attention comes from remarks made by Democrat John Box of Texas, one of the most vocal advocates of restricting Mexican immigration and extending national quotas to Mexico. Box questioned why Mexican immigration had become an issue in the debate over Johnson-Reed and insinuated that those charging that quotas had to be extended to Mexico or that Johnson-Reed should in some way tackle Mexican immigration had an ulterior motive. "I will say that I never heard of these gentlemen who oppose this bill making any objection to Mexican immigration in all the fight I have for years been making here against it," he said. "They are much concerned now when we are proposing to keep someone else out. I think that the record will show that some of these gentlemen who are complaining now voted against my every effort to keep them out at the time. They now want to kill this bill. I want the Mexicans kept out, but I do not want this bill killed by men who want these and all others admitted in unrestricted numbers" (65th Cong. Rec., 6132).

The concern on the part of some restrictionists, and one of the reasons why there was no serious push for quotas on Mexican immigration, according to Box's above statement, was that quotas on immigration from the Americas might be used to kill the Johnson-Reed bill. There was strong opposition on the part of agribusiness, as mentioned earlier, to any legislation that would limit the availability of labor in the Southwest. By the 1920s the Southwest was one of the most profitable agricultural regions in the United States and relied heavily on Mexican immigration (Hernandez 2010, 24).

Despite the lack of a strong push for restriction of Mexican immigration, numerous concerns were expressed regarding illegality and Mexican immigration during the debate over Johnson-Reed, as shown in table 1.4. As in the debate in the Senate, in the House debate more attention overall paid to Japanese immigration, and characterizations in the House matched those in the Senate, with the Japanese often portrayed as an economic or cultural threat. Illegality and criminality were only mentioned twice regarding the Japanese, while they were mentioned in ten separate comments by five different representatives regarding Mexicans.

In the House as in the Senate, the debate over Mexican immigrant criminality largely revolved around concerns that Mexican immigrants were disobeying existing immigration laws, for instance, not paying the

TABLE 1.4. Threat frames in the House Johnson-Reed debate: Unique mentions / number of representatives mentioning, by immigrant group

FRAME	JAPANESE	MEXICAN	ITALIAN
Positive economic	0/0	1/1	2/2
Negative economic	13/11	8/4	1/1
Positive cultural	5/5	0/0	2/2
Negative cultural	11/10	10/7	1/1
Positive criminal	0/0	0/0	1/1
Negative criminal	2/2	10/5	1/1

head tax. Democratic representative John E. Raker of California argued that the laws were not being enforced in regard to Mexican immigration; simply enforcing the laws, he said, would in and of itself reduce immigration from Mexico. Raker held that most Mexicans were illiterate, and thus ineligible to immigrate to the United States based on the Immigration Act of 1917, and that they often did not pay the required eight-dollar head tax. Under the contract labor law, per Raker, none of these individuals should have been admitted and thus "95% of all the Mexicans that come to the United States . . . have entered illegally" (65th Cong. Rec., 5842). He argued that of the approximately sixty thousand undocumented immigrants who entered the United States in 1924, only one thousand would have been allowed to enter had immigration laws been properly enforced. Yet what debate there was on undocumented Mexican immigration tended to focus not on the causal role of labor demands in the Southwest but on the lack of enforcement. A fellow Democrat, Representative Kunz of Illinois, asked, "Why not deport them? Chicago is being filled with Mexicans. Why not deport them if they are brought here illegally?" To which Raker replied, "We do not deport them because we have not got money enough" (65th Cong. Rec., 5887).

The inability of the Border Patrol to control immigration from Mexico was also a concern. Addressing undocumented immigration, Raker asked Representative Box to "state whether or not the testimony was not presented to our committee that hundreds of thousands came across the Mexican line fraudulently, and also swam the river—they were called wet backs—and the only thing that can keep them out is a proper patrolling of the border." Box responded that this was true (65th Cong. Rec., 6132). Democrat Adolph Sabath of Illinois had earlier pointed out that "it has been impossible for the Immigration Service to maintain an adequate patrol on the Mexican border because of lack of funds, thus opening the way for illegal entrance" (65th Cong. Rec., 5935). The tendency in the House, then, was to treat the undocumented entry of Mexicans not only as an issue of labor demands but as one of enforcement as well. An exchange between Representatives Sabath and Madden ended with Sabath declaring that "they [Mexicans] are a menace to the sections of the country to which they go," though he did not elaborate on what he meant by *menace*.

Some members of the House argued vociferously against quotas being imposed on European immigration, when Mexican immigration did not face any regulation beyond inspection and the head tax. Some believed that the reason for not imposing quotas on Mexican immigration was to facilitate the exploitation of the cheap labor it provided. Republican representative LaGuardia, of New York, pointed out that "the report of the Commissioner General of Immigration shows that 67,000 Mexicans entered the United States last year, also the Secretary of Labor has publicly stated that as many unlawfully entered. It is not disputed that several hundred thousands came in 1917 and 1918 and that they have not left the United States but are going from place to place where cheap labor is desired and where manufacturers or growers are specially calloused to want to exploit this peon at the expense of natives, yes, and of decent immigrants" (65th Cong. Rec., 5887). Representative Sabath similarly pointed out that not applying the quotas to Canada and Mexico gave those states bordering Mexico and Canada an unfair advantage because of their access to the labor both countries provided, both legal and illegal (65th Cong. Rec., 5935).

In the House debate, Mexican immigrants tended to be painted almost entirely as an economic threat, in part as a result of exploitation, as contract laborers were blamed for the deliberate and systematic import of illegal Mexican labor. The criminality of Mexican immigrants, outside of concerns about armed coyotes, was tied to the illegality of their entry rather than to any perception that Mexican immigrants were more inclined to criminality. Raker estimated that "over 90 percent of those Mexicans who come here come in violation of the law" (65th Cong. Rec., 6132). There were some attributions of criminality to Mexicans generally, though, and a table claiming to show the incarceration rate by nationality and racial group was inserted into the Congressional Record. In the table, Mexicans came in third in terms of criminality, and it was noted that the crimes covered were "the most degenerate and antisocial types of conduct" (65th Cong. Rec., 5680). Unsurprisingly, it was found that old immigrant stocks from northern and western Europe were less prone to criminality than newer stocks from Italy or Serbia. Curiously, while Mexican immigration was listed, it was not discussed, though the representative who had requested the table's insertion, Democrat Elton Watkins of Oregon, was using the table to make a point about southern and eastern European immigration rather than immigration from Mexico. This was largely indicative of the House debate, which dedicated less energy to Mexican immigration than had the Senate, instead focusing more on debate over European and, as in the Senate, Japanese immigration.

Johnson-Reed, Criminality, and Shifting Perceptions of Mexican Immigration

The passage of Johnson-Reed marked the beginning of a significant shift in perceptions of Mexican immigration. Johnson-Reed received overwhelming support in the House, where the vote was 323 to 71, as well as in the Senate, where it was 62 to 9. Seen initially as a relatively nonthreatening source of labor, by 1924 Mexican immigration had begun to be seen by some as potentially problematic. Despite this, limiting Mexican immigration because of concerns about crime, threats to jobs or wages, or assimilation was desired by a relatively small group of senators and representatives during debate on Johnson-Reed. Even those who favored applying quotas to Mexico feared that that might kill the bill because of the necessity of Mexican labor for the United States. The House and Senate differed in the frames most commonly used to argue against Mexican immigration and in terms of the commonality of positive framings. In the Senate, there were far more positive framings, and the cultural and economic threat of Mexican immigration was emphasized, with criminality coming in third among the threat frames often associated with immigration. There were some concerns about violence, but the concerns with the illegality of the immigrants themselves were greater. This latter concern with the unlawful presence of Mexican immigrants was echoed in the House, with concerns over illegality coming in second to negative cultural attributions. The House only had one positive framing of Mexican immigration, compared with fifteen in the Senate.

This notion of illegality is important because it would be the organizing principle for the handling of undocumented Mexican immigration. While the employers of undocumented immigrants were sometimes criticized, the emphasis was not on criminal treatment for those exploiting undocumented labor but rather for the immigrants themselves. The

Border Patrol treated undocumented immigration as a matter of criminal apprehension, and the tendency on the part of lawmakers to concentrate on the illegality of Mexican immigrants rather than on the employers exploiting them began the march toward the criminalization of undocumented immigration (Ngai 2003). In discussions of undocumented immigration during Johnson-Reed the focus was on the immigrants' violation of the border, their illiteracy, and their willingness to work for low wages. Undocumented immigrants, because of the very nature of their presence, bore almost sole responsibility for the "problem" of undocumented immigration. Employers were criticized but faced no penalties for their exploitation. In the hundreds of pages of debate on Johnson-Reed there was no evidence that Congress even considered penalties for employers as a possible solution.

Mexican Immigration after Johnson-Reed

Despite the inherent difficulties in restricting Mexican immigration, there was a push to apply quotas to the Western Hemisphere on the heels of the 1924 Johnson-Reed Act. This represented a realignment of restrictionist forces in Congress. Arguments about the racial inferiority of Mexican immigrants came to play a role in the debates over restriction. As noted earlier, American perceptions of Mexicans had long been colored by a certain racial paternalism, but restrictionists in the latter 1920s turned to narratives of racial threat to justify restriction.

On January 27, 1928, Democrat representative Robert A. Green of Florida delivered a speech over the radio that was subsequently entered into the Congressional Record. In this speech, Green noted, "Another reason why the quota should apply to any country south of the Rio Grande and the islands is because their population in the main is composed of mixture blood of White, Indian, and negro. This makes this blood a very great penalty upon the society which assimilates it. The United States already has sufficient race and blood troubles" (69th Cong. Rec., 2462). Representative John C. Box repeated this theme in an address he gave at an immigration conference, which he asked be entered into the Congressional Record during debate over quotas for Mexican immigration, arguing, "One purpose of our immigration laws is to prevent the lowering of the ideals and the average of our citizenship, the creation of race friction and the weakening of the Nation's powers of cohesion, resulting from the intermixing of differing races. The admission of 75,000 Mexican peons annually tends to the aggravation of this, another evil which the laws are designed to prevent or cure" (69th Cong.

Rec., 2818). Box had introduced bills beginning in 1926 that would have specifically applied quotas to Mexico and Latin America, but they had all died in committee.

These narratives of racial threat did not just tap into notions of inferiority and fears of miscegenation. By the latter part of the 1920s and the early 1930s there was also a focus on the potential criminality of Mexican immigrants as the flow of immigration from Europe was reduced and the United States headed into the Depression. Representative Box explicitly linked undocumented Mexican immigration to crime in his immigration conference address, stating, "The protection of American society against the importation of crime and pauperism is yet another object of these laws. Few, if any, other immigrants have brought us so large a proportion of criminals and paupers as have the Mexican peons" (69th Cong. Rec, 2818). During a Senate hearing on several bills that would have restricted or eliminated Mexican immigration, Edward H. Dowell, the vice president of the California Federation of Labor and a member of the city council of San Diego, gave testimony in which he drew heavily on the criminality frame to justify quotas. Mr. Dowell used the example of the prison population of San Quentin to highlight Mexican criminality: "There are in the California State penitentiary at San Quentin, 3,358 prisoners. Of that number 438 are Mexicans. In other words, about one-twelfth of the population of California are Mexicans and about one-seventh of the prison population are Mexican. Data supplied with the above figures shows that at least 60 percent of the violations of prison laws and rules in that penitentiary were credited to those few Mexicans that were in there" (*Restriction of Western Hemisphere Immigration* 1928, 10).

Dowell's testimony was the exception rather than the rule, with most of those asked to testify supportive of both the need for Mexican labor and the character of Mexican immigrants. In his testimony before the committee as a representative of the American Cattle Raisers Association, Fred H. Bixby said of his own experiences with Mexican immigrants, "I have a family—three of them are girls. Ever since they were that high [indicating] I have had them out on the range, riding the range with Mexicans, and they have been just as safe as if they had been with me. That is the kind of people who are working for me, and they are Mexicans. Do you suppose we would send them out with a bunch of negroes?" (*Restriction of Western Hemisphere Immigration* 1928, 30). Many other individuals brought before the committee commented on the good moral character of Mexican immigrants or the lack of threat they posed to American workers. Despite this, criminality was still a concern for members of Congress and the president, to the extent that a National Commission on Law Observance and Enforcement, formed in 1929 by President Herbert Hoover, specifically examined the criminality of Mexican immigrants.

The 1931 report of the eleven-member committee, which focused on identifying the causes of criminal activity, noted that despite statistics suggesting otherwise, the foreign born were frequently portrayed as being more inclined toward criminality. It also dedicated a whole section to examining the criminality of Mexican immigrants, finding that there was no conclusive evidence that Mexican immigrants were any more inclined toward criminality than were native whites (NCLOE 1931). A comment published in the *Michigan Law Review* in the same year stated that the findings of the report "show that the continued indictment for criminality of those just arrived is as old as the history of our country, and has been directed, during each period, with greatest vehemence against that national group whose migration here has been most recent and most marked. The Irish, Germans, Italians, and Mexicans, to mention only some of the outstanding cases, have each in turn been charged with a high susceptibility to crime" (Cohen 1931, 99). The report also pointed out that racial prejudice directed at Mexicans could very well play a role in these charges (NCLOE 1931, 412). The report by the Wickersham Commission was released too late to be considered during debate over S. 5094, but the fact that it dedicated an entire portion of the report to examining the criminality of Mexican immigrants shows that this was a concern in the lead-up to the bill's passage.

In addition to the threats of race-mixing and criminality, both Box and Harris, as well as other members of Congress, pushed the idea of Mexican immigration as a threat to American laborers. It was argued that Mexican laborers drove down wages and took the jobs of US workers, as well as being a burden on social services and charitable societies. Democrat Eugene Black of Texas expressed his support for the Box Bill, which would have amended the Johnson-Reed Act to include Mexico in national quotas in order to protect American labor from unrestricted Mexican immigration. He stated that he took this position not because of racial prejudice or any ill will toward the Mexican people but simply because he believed it was in the best interests of American citizens (69th Cong. Rec., 2860). Box commented multiple times about the threat posed to the American worker by Mexican immigrants, as did Senator Harris, with the former combining the economic threat from Mexican immigrants with narratives of racial inferiority, criminality, and disease in pushing for strict limits (69th Cong. Rec., 2817).

While discussion of the illegality of Mexican immigration and some information on violence associated with coyotes, the smugglers who helped Mexican immigrants enter the United States, had been entered into the Congressional Record in 1924, the explicit language of criminality had rarely been used in discussions of undocumented immigration. However, what had started as a discussion focused primarily on the illegality on Mexican immigrants quickly shifted to one that linked this illegality to criminality. As demonstrated in the preceding quotations, by 1928 members of Congress had begun to use criminality as one of the justifications for restriction and increased border security. In the Johnson-Reed debate, Box had focused on the illegality of Mexican immigrants, but later he had shifted to characterizing the "Mexican peons" as criminals, and not just for their violation of US immigration law. This shift is important because the modern convergence of immigration and criminal law relies heavily on the narrative of the "criminal immigrant," someone who is a threat to American citizens for reasons beyond how they entered the United States.

The attempt on the part of some to paint Mexican immigrants as criminals and a cultural and economic threat in the post-Johnson-Reed period was met with resistance. A number of Colorado chambers of commerce and agricultural interests sent in resolutions to Congress noting their opposition to the restriction of Mexican immigration. Many of these resolutions noted the dependency of Colorado agricultural interests (particularly the sugar beet industry) on Mexican labor and the positive characteristics of the Mexican workers (69th Cong. Rec., 1153–57). In congressional testimony, E. J. Walker, of the Arizona Cotton Growers Association, noted, "It should be further realized in discussing this question that the four border states were at one time largely a part of Mexico and that from a geographic and climatic standpoint they naturally form a proper background for the Mexican and that this class of labor is as essential to the economic welfare of these States as is the colored labor to the South and Northeast" (*Restriction of Western Hemisphere Immigration* 1928, 36). Many members of Congress similarly opposed the restriction of Mexican immigration, with Representative Olger Burtness, a Republican from North Dakota, arguing that Mexican immigrants posed no threat to American labor, though he noted that he was not arguing that they were the best people on earth, just that they were necessary for agriculture (69th Cong. Rec., 8467). Attempts to apply quotas to immigration from the Western Hemisphere were ultimately thwarted by "Southern Democrats and Western lawmakers who relied on cheap Mexican labor" who recognized the labor issues that would be faced in the Southwest if access to Mexican workers was severely restricted (Tichenor 2002, 146). During congressional hearings on quotas, many also questioned whether American workers would do the jobs currently done by Mexicans if this labor supply was suddenly cut off. A. C. Hardinson, who represented the California State Grange and Farmers' Union, argued that there was a "certain type of work" that Americans simply would not do, work that was nonetheless necessary to maintain the United States' economic position in the world (*Restriction of Western Hemisphere Immigration* 1928, 47). The exact same argument—that most Americans will simply not take the kinds of jobs Mexican workers typically come here to do—continues to be made today. The same forces that resisted quotas would ensure that restrictions on legal Mexican immigration were not passed until the 1970s.

As the economy of the United States began to slip toward the Great Depression, both the public and members of Congress began to see Mexican immigration as more of a threat (Tichenor 2001). While there were no quota restrictions, Mexican immigrants could be excluded through administrative means and the enforcement of existing provisions of immigration law. Greater enforcement of the ban on contract labor, the literacy test, and the exclusion of any likely to become a public charge reduced Mexican immigration between the late 1920s and the early 1930s. Restriction was also attempted via administrative means, such as increases in the head tax and a requirement that Mexican immigrants subject themselves to humiliating delousing baths (Ngai 2004). Mexican immigration dropped from 58,747 a year in the late 1920s to 12,703 in 1930 because of these changes in enforcement (Ngai 1999, 90). Yet this decrease in immigration did not account for undocumented immigration from Mexico, which remained largely unaddressed despite the formation of the Border Patrol in 1924. With the existing resistance to quotas on Mexican immigration, restrictionists had to be satisfied with reducing Mexican immigration through greater enforcement of existing immigration law and a push to criminalize undocumented immigration. The second half of the 1920s was thus marked by increasing hostility toward Mexican immigration generally, with the Border Patrol deployed solely along the southern border and the increasing use of administrative means to reduce legal Mexican immigration. This hostility to Mexican immigration would culminate in the passage of S. 5094 in 1929.

The Undesirable Aliens Act of 1929

Senate bill 5094 was introduced on December 22, 1928, by Democrat Coleman Blease of South Carolina, a known white supremacist, and referred to the Committee on Immigration (B. Simon 1996). The bill sought to criminalize undocumented entry, making crossing into the United States without inspection a misdemeanor, punishable by one year in prison, a fine of one thousand dollars, or both. Undocumented reentry after deportation would be a felony under the act, punishable by two years in prison, a thousand-dollar fine, or both. Reentry, because it carried a felony charge, would also make the immigrant in question ineligible for future immigration to the United States, as felons were not admissible under US immigration policy.

S. 5094, also called the Undesirable Aliens Act in congressional debate, was reported out of committee on January 18, 1929 (70th Cong. Rec., 3542). The committee's report included a memorandum from the Labor Department stating that "it frequently happens that aliens of the criminal and other classes who are deported under the general immigration law reenter the country unlawfully" (US Senate Committee on Immigration 1929). Included in the same report was a letter from Secretary of Labor James Davis noting that without a deterrent penalty for reentry there was little hope of dissuading those who were deported from attempting reentry (US Senate Committee on Immigration 1929). The hearing of the House Committee on Immigration and Naturalization included a specific mention of the criminalization of undocumented immigration under S. 5094 that was part of a memorandum from the American Civil Liberties Union arguing against passage of the bill (*Certificates of Arrival* 1929). The ACLU found the bill "especially objectionable in making criminal an illegal entry into the United States." "It is one thing," the ACLU continued, "to deport a person for coming here illegally; it is quite another thing to imprison for a year or fine him a thousand dollars, especially as he might be quite ignorant of the law when he starts his journey" (*Certificates of Arrival* 1929). The ACLU's objection to S. 5094 was based on section 2 of the bill, which stated, "Any alien who hereafter enters the United States at any time or place other than as designated by immigration officials or eludes examination or inspection by immigration officials, or obtains entry into the United States by a willfully false or misleading representation or the willful concealment of any material fact, shall be guilty of a misdemeanor and, upon conviction, shall be punished by imprisonment for not more than one year or by a fine of not more than $1,000, or by both such fine and imprisonment." For those who had already been deported, the penalty was higher: "If any alien has been arrested and deported in pursuance of law, he shall be excluded from admission into the United States. . . . If he enters or attempts to enter the United States after the expiration of sixty days after the enactment of this Act, he shall be guilty of a felony and upon conviction . . . be punished by imprisonment for not more than two years or by a fine of not more than $1,000, or by both such fine and imprisonment" (Immigration Act of March 4th, 1929).

The House had initially tried to make the bill more far-reaching by including provisions to deport foreign born associated with the white slave trade, violations of the narcotics act, or violations of law carrying a sentence of two years or more or conviction for two or more offenses (*Certificates of Arrival* 1929). An additional amendment to the bill introduced by Representative Tarver of Georgia would have also allowed aliens to be deported for bootlegging (70th Cong. Rec., 3615). In debate, Representative Sabath noted that many of the violators of the Volstead Act, which prohibited the sale or manufacture of alcohol, were in fact US citizens, adding, "Unlike the gentlemen from Georgia, Florida, Washington or Maine I am frank enough to admit that there are many violators of the prohibition law in my state and city" (70th Cong. Rec., 3616). When S. 5094 passed, it included none of these provisions, instead dealing only with penalties for those reentering the United States after deportation or those entering without inspection. As such, it specifically targeted Mexican immigration. The passage of S. 5094 effectively criminalized undocumented immigration for the first time in US history, making illegal entry not simply a deportable offense but one that carried criminal penalties. S. 5094 intertwined the rhetoric of criminality, which had long been used against the foreign born generally, and the legal treatment of immigrants. Undocumented reentrants were not only illegal; they were now felons. While some European nationals had previously been scapegoated with an eye to restricting their entry into the United States, at no time prior to this had the very act of immigration itself been criminalized in such a fashion. This separated Latino immigrants, and Mexicans more specifically, from past immigrant groups, who had been demonized but not treated as criminals under the law, regardless of how they entered the country. It also made those deported for a crime ineligible for reentry and allowed them to be charged with a felony for reentry after deportation, as was the case with undocumented immigrants.

Framing Immigration: S. 5094 in Congress

S. 5094 was uncontroversial enough that there was little debate over the bill in the Senate, where it was introduced. After it was reported out of committee, Representative Blease brought the bill before the Senate on January 23, 1929, and it promptly passed after one minor amendment to the language was agreed upon (70th Cong. Rec., 2092). The vote was not recorded for S. 5094, suggesting strong support during the voice vote, which is not surprising given the content of the bill. S. 5094 was not aimed at limiting legal Mexican immigration, which, as discussed earlier was controversial, but instead focused specifically on using criminal penalties to deter undocumented entry, legally linking illegality and criminality formally in the way it was already linked in the minds of many members of Congress.

Because of the lack of Senate debate, I draw on only the House in discussing the characterization of undocumented immigrants and the threat frames used in pushing for the passage of the bill. Even the House debate was given fewer than forty pages in the Congressional Record, compared with the more than three hundred pages for the House debate on Johnson-Reed, though the latter was of course a much more complex piece of legislation. Again, this drives home how uncontroversial criminalizing undocumented immigration was at the time, particularly compared with the modern immigration debate, in which criminalization is a central feature. Because of the limited time given to debate over S. 5094, as well as the fact that most of this debate was focused on the various amendments, the number of threat frames drawn upon was very limited. This made quantifying them in the manner of the Johnson-Reed debate of little value, though there was enough material to allow for a discussion of how Mexican immigration was framed when it was mentioned specifically.

When debate for S. 5094 was opened alongside three other bills relating to immigration in the House, including the Box Bill, which would have applied quotas to Canada and Mexico, Democrat John J. O'Connor of New York noted the racial undertones of S. 5094 and the warped vision of America that it presented. In a long speech, O'Connor argued, "I fear there is a spirit pervading our country today reflected in these immigration bills that is a menace to the country—a spirit of intolerance and bigotry not only to religions but to races. . . . Has anyone here ever said anything about establishing a penal colony for the deportation of citizen criminals and the putting out of the country the criminal citizen?" He later continued, ""How long can demagogues in all political parties continue to preach this doctrine of saying "America for Americans only" and further foment this vindictive intolerance evidenced by these bills? It surely must result in damage to our country. It is a spirit of vindictiveness against anybody whose ancestors were not born here 300 years ago. I do not care what its effect is in elections, but I do care what effect it is going to have on our country in the future." (70th Cong. Rec., 3526). S. 5094 was, without question, about Mexican immigration, and more specifically undocumented Mexican immigration, though it technically could apply to European or Asian immigrants as well. This is reflected in the number of times Mexicans were mentioned in the House debate over the bills, with the terms *Mexican* and *Mexicans* being used with greater regularity than any other national or regional identifiers. Mexicans were mentioned more than three times as often as the next national or regional group. This contrasts with the number of mentions in the House debate over the Johnson-Reed Act, where mentions of Mexicans came in seventh overall.

Criminality was brought up on a number of occasions during debate over S. 5094. In the House, Representative Green noted that there were an estimated one million aliens in the United States who had entered illegally and that "if you will examine the criminal records you will find that, in proportion to alien population, the percentage of criminals is largely foreign" (70th Cong. Rec., 3547). Republican John C. Schafer of Wisconsin challenged Green on this directly: "His speech indicates that only criminals are aliens. I would like to see him amend his views as to be willing to deport the notorious criminals in the Klu-Klux Klan organization" (70th Cong. Rec., 3548). While Green did not specifically mention Mexican immigrants as the source of this criminality, his statements were later echoed by Box, a longtime proponent of restricting Mexican immigration.

As mentioned earlier, Box had introduced one bill after another attempting to amend the Johnson-Reed Act to include quotas for Mexican immigration, though these ultimately failed in committee (Hoffman 1974, 24). Box went beyond just painting Mexican immigrants as criminals, though: "They are badly infected with tuberculosis and other diseases; there are many paupers among them; there are many criminals; they work for lower wages; they are objectionable as immigrants when tried by the tests applied to other aliens." Box also believed that Mexican immigrants constituted a threat to racial harmony in the United States, stating that through the continued admission of Mexican laborers (legally and otherwise) the United States was "breeding another one of those great race questions" (70th Cong. Rec., 3620). Following this statement, Representative Roy Fitzgerald, a Republican from Ohio, chimed in that Mexicans were "poisoning the American citizen" (70th Cong. Rec., 3620). These statements regarding Mexicans were not applied to Europeans or Canadians entering illegally across the northern border, though the law applied equally to them. Additionally, Box's comments regarding the immigration of Mexicans "raising a serious race question" (70th Cong. Rec., 3619) reveal the racism that drove much of the desire to limit both legal and illegal Mexican immigration in 1929.

The economic threat frame was also used in arguing for the passage of S. 5094, citing the threat cheap Mexican labor posed to American workers. Schafer noted that "these Mexicans also come into Wisconsin in droves, and take the places of American citizens in the factories and on the farm. Often we see the spectacle of war veterans walking the streets unable to obtain employment because of the unfair competition of cheap Mexican labor." Representative Thomas Blanton of Texas sardonically asked in response, "Why does not the energetic, enterprising 300-pound member from Wisconsin put some of his energy into action along that line and stop it?" (70th Cong. Rec., 3619). Blanton went on to explicitly mention undocumented Mexican immigrants as a reason to include an amendment declaring reentry a felony, arguing that if undocumented immigration was not stopped, "we are going to have Americans starving to death in the Hoover administration" (70th Cong. Rec., pg. 3619). This statement, while addressing the economic threat potentially posed by undocumented labor, also suggests that undocumented immigration could be responsible for American deaths, even if indirectly. S. 5094 passed both chambers in 1929, becoming Public Law 1018. No vote was recorded in the House or the Senate on S. 5094. It marked the culmination of a crackdown on Mexican immigration that had begun in 1924 with the formation of the Border Patrol and would lead to a program of Mexican repatriation between 1929 and 1939. The passage of S. 5094 meant that undocumented entry was now a misdemeanor, punishable by one year in prison and a fine of one thousand dollars, and reentry a felony, punishable by two years in prison and a thousand-dollar fine; and it made the offending immigrant ineligible for future legal immigration. For the first time, to be illegal was also to be a criminal, reinforcing the longstanding rhetorical linkage between the two.

Driven in part by the Depression, both S. 5094 and Mexican Repatriation, an Immigration and Naturalization Services (INS) program aimed at encouraging Mexican nationals to return to Mexico, helped to create a climate of fear, complete with rumors of immigration raids and fines, to encourage Mexican aliens to "voluntarily" repatriate (Hoffman 1974). This resulted in the out-migration of approximately five hundred thousand Mexicans over a ten-year period (Ngai 2004). While there were no limits on Mexican immigration until 1976, S. 5094, together with the Mexican Repatriation, locked in two trends that would henceforth be part of US immigration policy. First, there was the conflation of undocumented status with criminality beyond simple illegality, which had begun with the formation of the Border Patrol and passage of Johnson-Reed in 1924. This legitimized the longstanding rhetorical linkage between criminality and the foreign born, while also formalizing the status of the undocumented as criminals. The Undesirable Aliens Act also instituted the adversarial relationship between the US government and Mexican laborers, despite the reliance of US industries on these very individuals. While undocumented labor continued to be used with regularity by employers in the United States, those working these jobs were now subject not only to deportation but also to potential fines and jail time. Criminalization also gave undocumented immigrants little recourse if they were mistreated or exploited, making them as Ngai so aptly puts it "impossible subjects" (Ngai 2004).

The Political Policy Legacy of S. 5094

S. 5094 was passed forty-seven years before Mexican immigration became subject to immigration quotas in 1976 and fifty-seven years before undocumented immigration was comprehensively addressed for the first time via IRCA. This decision to formally criminalize undocumented entry, while using the rhetoric of criminality to describe undocumented immigration, locked in the treatment of undocumented immigration as a criminal act. In addition, it further separated Mexican immigrants from other groups in that Mexican immigrants' presence in the United States was the first to be criminalized. The racial undertones of this criminalization were clear both in the debate over S. 5094 itself and in comments by men like Representative Box, as well as in the decision to deploy the Border Patrol solely along the Mexican border in 1924. In the fifty-seven years between S. 5094 and IRCA, the Border Patrol was expanded multiple times and the INS expanded interior enforcement through initiatives like Operation Wetback in 1954, which resembled a crime-control operation in its frequent raids of workplaces and neighborhoods (Garcia 1980; Ngai 2004). The treatment of undocumented immigration as a crime-control issue would influence media coverage, with the focal point becoming arrests and raids. Media imagery, even today, frequently pairs stories on undocumented immigration with footage of immigrants being apprehended and handcuffed (Drier and Tabak 2009; Kim et al. 2011).

The racial project of criminalization that began in the 1920s would set the standard for the treatment of undocumented immigrants. When undocumented crossing first became illegal under the Immigration Act of 1917, while it was nothing more than an administrative violation, its construction as illegal suggested a solution in line with other illegal activity, deterrence through punishment. S. 5094 brought together the mental construction of undocumented immigrants as a criminals, on the basis of on their violation of the border, and their legal treatment. Undocumented immigration was no longer just illegal; it now was criminal and potentially marked the immigrant as a felon.

As discussed in the introduction, path dependence plays a significant role in the development of policy. Because of this, even small events in the early part of a process, such as the criminalization of undocumented immigration in 1929, may have a greater impact than those that come later. Thus, the criminalization of Mexican immigration in 1929 and the launching of Mexican Repatriation that same year made alternative solutions, such as criminalizing the hiring of illegal workers, less likely. Any change deemphasizing crime-control tactics would constitute a new approach entailing costs, both financial and political, as well as uncertain results. One of the greatest benefits of criminalization is that it entailed far fewer potential costs than did alternative solutions. Even if it failed to truly address undocumented immigration, politicians could point to raids, deportations, and "voluntary" repatriation as signs of success.

As Orren and Skowronek (2004) have argued, politics is always the result of previous paths taken or choices made. S. 5094 was itself the result of increasingly restrictionist policies on immigration that had first led to the Chinese Exclusion Act, then to the Asiatic Barred Zone, and finally to Johnson-Reed. Each of these victories emboldened restrictionists and made a liberalization of immigration policy, which would not be seen until the 1950s and 1960s, much more difficult. S. 5094 was signed into law during a period of increasing hostility to Mexican immigrants and started the United States on a trajectory toward increasing criminalization in two ways. First, there was an emphasis on law enforcement as the first and only real answer to undocumented immigration. Members of the House, in debating Johnson-Reed, focused on the need to increase the number of Border Patrol agents and to enforce existing immigration policies such as the literacy test and head taxes. This rhetoric of enforcement and illegality led five years after Johnson-Reed to the passage of S. 5094 and the beginning of the convergence of immigration and criminal law. Second, there was no attempt by Congress to address the labor demands that led to undocumented immigration or to place some responsibility on employers. There would be no real attempt to address labor demands and the effect they had on undocumented immigration until the beginning of the Bracero Program in 1942, and there would be no employer sanctions until IRCA was passed in 1986. Instead, the bulk of the responsibility was placed on the immigrants themselves, while allowing employers to continue their exploitation of Mexican labor. The laborers would be spoken of as criminals and rhetorically referred to as "illegals" or "wetbacks" for a large part of the nation's history.

S. 5094 was important because it occurred very early in the policy process of immigration control, at a time when control of the southern border was just emerging as an issue in American politics. It was a time when immigration restriction was at its zenith, when Asians were for the most part completely excluded and southern or eastern Europeans faced strict quotas. The success of immigration restriction in 1924 led to Mexican immigration, and undocumented immigration, landing on the congressional agenda for the first time as restrictionists turned from Asian and "undesirable" European immigration to another immigrant group that was perceived as problematic. The tendency to deal with undocumented immigration in a patchwork fashion emphasizing deportation and deterrence through punishment became locked in and the norm until passage of IRCA, which itself was driven largely by an increasing public awareness of undocumented immigration and a desire to see it addressed (Tichenor 2002). Millions of Mexican immigrants were labeled illegal in the decades between the passage of S. 5094 and IRCA, a status that forced these communities into the shadows and made programs like Mexican Repatriation and Operation Wetback acceptable to both politicians and the public. Both relied on immigration raids and the threat of fines or arrest to drive "voluntary" repatriation, while also solidifying the adversarial relationship between undocumented workers and the American government. Undocumented immigrants were criminals, having violated the sovereignty of the United States and broken its immigration laws, often deliberately. Little mention was made of the role of employers, who avoided the label of criminality so liberally applied to generations of laborers who contributed to the economic prosperity of the United States.

TWO

From the Path Less Traveled to the Path Best Known

In Chapter 1 I argued that S. 5094 forged the formal linkage between the rhetoric of criminality and the legal treatment of immigrants that led to the criminalization of the undocumented. Drawing on theories of path dependence, I posited that this, along with increasing hostility toward Mexican immigrants in the 1920s, set that the United States on a path on which the tools used to address crime control became the primary "solution" to undocumented immigration. The criminal penalties associated with undocumented entry and reentry under S. 5094 entrenched deterrence through the punishment of the immigrant, leaving the employer untouched. To justify this, the potential criminality of Mexican immigrants was frequently cited in congressional debate, as were cultural and economic threat frames that painted them as unassimilable and a threat to American labor, respectively. In the period following the passage of S. 5094, attempts to address undocumented immigration would be relatively haphazard, with no push for comprehensive reform. Instead, a piecemeal approach was taken, with deportation campaigns (Mexican Repatriation and Operation Wetback) as well as an attempt to address labor demands through the Bracero Program. The 1980s would mark the beginning of an era of increasing media attention to and rising concern on the part of the public about undocumented immigration, which led to the passage of IRCA in 1986.

IRCA represented a unique opportunity in the history of undocumented immigration in the United States. Because of growing frustration with the failure of deterrent penalties and an acknowledgment by government officials of both the value and the necessity of Mexican labor, for the first time the focus of immigration enforcement shifted from the immigrants alone to include employers. IRCA granted amnesty to millions of immigrants who had been working in the United States and established a guest-worker program in hopes of meeting labor demands. Employer sanctions became a part of immigration legislation for the first time, with deterrence now aimed not only at the immigrant through the Border Patrol, the INS, and the threat of charges and deportation but also at the employers who profited from their labor. IRCA introduced legal responsibilities for employers and a verification system that was meant to reduce the hiring of undocumented laborers. Criminalization was not absent from IRCA. There was additional funding for border control and internal enforcement, as well as stricter penalties for harboring undocumented workers or facilitating their presence in the United States. The expansion of the Border Patrol would increase the militarization of the southern border, even though this expansion did not reflect the volume of undocumented immigration in any way (Massey 2007). Criminalization was not the sole focus of IRCA, which was a significant shift, and one that has not been repeated in immigration policy. IRCA's promised new path for immigration never became a reality, for a few reasons.

One of IRCA's main problems was the loopholes for hiring undocumented workers, since fines were only levied if the undocumented immigrant was employed directly, allowing many to sidestep potential financial penalties by hiring labor through contractors. These contractors were responsible for hiring the immigrants and verifying their employment eligibility before contracting them out to agricultural interests. There was also a good faith clause that employers only had to see a set of documents proving work eligibility, not make sure that they were in fact legitimate (Tichenor 2002). Thus, employers could continue hiring undocumented workers as long as they used a contractor who could provide documents showing that the workers were eligible to work in the United States.

The second problem with immigration reform under IRCA was in its guest-worker program, which was too difficult to navigate and did not sufficiently address labor demands. The border remained porous, making true border control an impossibility and making the red tape surrounding the guest-worker program unnecessary to navigate, since employers could continue to rely on undocumented immigration obtained through contractors (Tichenor 2002). This allowed for greater flexibility in terms of the work force, which was available when needed, and eliminated the need to wait on government approval or certification to bring in workers.

The final problem was that the increase in the militarization of the

southern border under IRCA made it less likely that undocumented immigrants would return to Mexico, which had been the institutionalized
pattern for the decades following the passage of S. 5094. Avoiding the
Border Patrol became more difficult with the increase in officers, and
as a result border crossing became more difficult and expensive (Massey
2007). This would contribute to the near doubling of the undocumented
population between 1986 and 1996 (see fig. A1).

IRCA did grant legal status to millions, but therein lies the central
problem of IRCA. While the amnesty program was a success, all the other
parts of the bill failed to reduce the influx of undocumented immigrants.
The critical failure of IRCA would lead to a return to deterrence through
criminalization under the Illegal Immigration Reform and Immigrant
Responsibility Act (IIRIRA) in 1996. IRCA's failure also delegitimized its
primary success in amnesty, which came to be seen as simply rewarding
those who broke the law, while doing little to address undocumented
immigration. As discussed in the introduction, *critical policy failures* are
policies that attempt a significant shift in how a particular policy problem is addressed and conceptualized, therefore carrying a heavy burden
for failure. The failure of these policies can delegitimize the new approach
attempted and make a regression to the previously existing path likely.

Prohibition provides an excellent example of a critical policy failure
that was similar, in some ways, to IRCA. Prior to the ratification of the
Eighteenth Amendment, alcohol had been legal in the United States,
but concerns about abuse, driven by the Anti-Saloon League, led to its
becoming illegal in the United States (Clark 1976). The ratification of
the Eighteenth Amendment was a drastic departure from the past and a
critical failure. Despite Prohibition, Americans continued to drink, and
a black market grew up around alcohol production to ensure a supply.
Ultimately, the US government would concede its inability to regulate
the consumption of alcohol, and the Twenty-First Amendment would
end Prohibition in 1933. As with IRCA, the result of Prohibition's failure
was a return to the previous policy path. Alcohol was legal once again,
just as in the post-IRCA period undocumented immigration came to be
criminalized once again.

The shift back to criminal penalties and increasing criminalization
under IIRIRA was owing in part to the United States' long history of
criminalization as a solution to undocumented immigration. Again, over
fifty-seven years the Border Patrol was increased in size, the goal of the
INS became the apprehension and deportation of undocumented immigrants, and perhaps more importantly, undocumented immigration

became almost inextricably linked to criminality in the minds of many legislators and the American public. During this period, the Bracero Program, the Texas Proviso, and the Hart-Cellar Act all helped exacerbate the issues that contributed to undocumented immigration. When the attempted pivot to a new way of dealing with undocumented immigration came up short, it was easy to return to the course that was well known and much more safe politically, as well as politically ripe for the right wing of the GOP. Blame was shifted back to the immigrant, and policy regressed back to a simple focus on crime control, in which fences and increases in the size of the Border Patrol and the INS could be sold as being tough on illegal immigration.

In the pages that follow, I examine two questions concerning IRCA and IIRIRA. First, what role did criminality play in the debates on these laws, and did they differ from each other and from the debates over the Johnson-Reed Act and S. 5094? Second, what role did these two policies play in furthering the convergence between immigration and criminal law? I argue that IRCA represented a moment of punctuated equilibrium in which restrictionist forces for the first time lost ground in immigration policy because of the continuing problem of undocumented immigration, the failure of criminal penalties, and a conservative administration that valued the labor of undocumented immigrants. This is reflected both in the frames referenced in the IRCA debate and in its policy prescriptions. I also argue that IRCA represented a critical policy failure because it failed to slow undocumented immigration, leading to a reentrenchment of criminalization as congressional policy. This was demonstrated in the passage of IIRIRA in 1996, in which much of the discourse once again hinged on the rhetoric of immigrant criminality.

After S. 5094: The Wickersham Commission and Mexican Criminality

While there had been a focus on the criminality of Mexican immigrants in the debate on S. 5094, no statistics had been included to support the assertions of criminality. However, just a few years after S. 5094 was passed, the National Commission on Law Observance and Enforcement (NCLOE) published a lengthy report on this very question. The Report on Crime and the Foreign Born, published in 1931, looked at immigrant criminality among the foreign born but also included a separate section on Mexican immigration specifically, as well as a number of individual case studies of specific cities. As mentioned earlier, Mexican immigration, particularly undocumented immigration due to the porousness of the border, had become more of a national issue between 1920 and 1930 (Nevins 2010). NCLOE would come to be known by the name of its chairman, George W. Wickersham, and is commonly referred to as the Wickersham Commission, though for the sake of brevity, the abbreviation NCLOE will be used here.

The NCLOE report is worth considering at length because of the great perspective it provides not only on thinking at the time regarding the foreign born but also on the reality of Mexican criminality when it was being problematized for the first time. What is particularly striking about the report is that it takes a very neutral approach, acknowledged in the introductory statement, which notes that immigrant criminality "is a subject that is clouded with prejudice" and "has rarely been subject to impartial, disinterested inquiry" (NCLOE 1931, 11). The report notes that there are "two aspects" to the question of immigrant criminality. The first is whether there is a criminal element among the foreign born, which does not assume that one nationality is more predisposed toward crime. To use a modern example, are there drug-cartel members in the flow of immigration from Mexico? While this still qualifies as scapegoating, it is milder than the second aspect the report considers, which is whether certain national groups have greater criminal tendencies than others. Again, to use a modern example, are Mexican immigrants more likely to break the law than Ukrainian immigrants solely because of their ethnic identity? This belief presupposes that criminality is more inherent to certain ethnic groups and not necessarily just the result of external circumstances such as high rates of poverty. The report acknowledged that the immigrant-as-criminal narrative had been around since the colonial period: "The theory that immigration is responsible for crime, that the most recent 'wave of immigration,' whatever the nationality, is less desirable than the old ones, that all newcomers should be regarded with an attitude of suspicion, is a theory almost as old as the colonies planted by Englishmen on the New England coast" (NCLOE 1931, 23). The report went on to discuss some potential reasons for this conflation of foreignness with criminality, linking it to the early use of transportation by the Crown as well as the likelihood that many "black sheep of good families" had been sent to America to get rid of them (NCLOE 1931). Thus, even in 1931 there was an understanding that these linkages were as old as the United States itself and the result of both nativism and racism, as well as the practice of transportation, which in some cases may have justified the suspicion of the foreign born in these earlier times.

Before turning to a discussion of Mexican immigration specifically, the report spends a great deal of time examining the question whether the foreign born were more likely to engage in criminal behavior than the native born and the reasons for this suspicion. The report looks not only at immigration in the twentieth century but also at attitudes toward the foreign born in both the colonial period and the nineteenth century, when recent immigrants were believed to be responsible for more crime than the native born. It is also pointed out that these attitudes had always seemed to correspond with waves of immigration. While older generations of immigrants were regarded as boons to the nation, newer immigrants were regularly portrayed as prone to criminality, either because of inherent characteristics or because of deliberate malfeasance on the part of European governments who conspired to send criminals and the worst of their citizens to America (NCLOE 1931, 23–44). The evidence presented to prove the criminality of these immigrants was usually in the form of arrest rates or incarceration for foreign born in a handful of locations. For instance, the New York Association for Improving the Condition of the Poor in 1859 reported that immigrants from Ireland constituted 55 percent of all those arrested in New York City, compared with 23 percent for the native born Americans (NCLOE 1931, 40). However, even if these percentages were true, a number of factors could have played a role in the increased arrest rate for the Irish in New York City that had nothing to do with an inherent criminality, such as understanding of the law or poverty. Similar circumstantial evidence would be presented on the floor of Congress during debate over S. 5094 to argue that Mexican immigrants, like the Irish before them, were predisposed to criminality.

The NCLOE report notes the importance of considering the context in which criminality is discussed. In fact, instead of laying blame solely at the feet of the immigrant population, the report asks, "When a man or woman has established a bona fide domicile in this country, marries, and sets up an American home and becomes the parent of American children, and after a period of years in this country becomes criminal, or prostitute, or anarchist, does not the responsibility belong to this country rather than his early home?" (NCLOE 1931, 69). This suggestion that context matters, and that the perceived criminality of the immigrant population in the United States may be based on conditions here, rather than either an inherent criminality or a larger number of criminals in the immigrant community, is repeated throughout the report. The report later discusses differences in culture, language, and poverty rates as potential reasons for increased criminality on the part of the foreign born in some locations. Viewed as a whole, though, even the secondary evidence from the period preceding the report, which NCLOE considers in detail, suggests that "immigrants are less prone to commit crime than native-born Americans" (NCLOE 1931, 71). This finding contradicts those of the earlier Dillingham Commission, which found higher rates of criminality among immigrant groups, though as was discussed earlier, there were some issues with the commission's methodology.

If there were no concrete linkages between immigration and crime in the period preceding the NCLOE report, what about during the early 1930s, when the report was published? S. 5094 had been passed just two years earlier, and the rate of immigrant criminality in 1931 likely would have varied little from the rate in 1929. Debate over S. 5094 had centrally featured the immigrant-as-criminal narrative as a justification for felony charges for illegal reentrants as congressional attention turned away from the much-maligned European nationalities to Mexicans. This was owing in large part to the successful passage of the Johnson-Reed Act, which significantly reduced rates of immigration from "undesirable" European countries. This shift from the former targets of the immigrant-as-criminal narrative to Mexicans is specifically noted in the NCLOE report, which states that throughout US history there has been an attempt to attribute criminality to specific groups, and "now this criticism is directed toward the Mexican" (NLCOE 1931, 72). The report points out that Mexicans were preceded by Italians, who were in turn preceded by the Irish.

After examining the evidence for criminality among the foreign born in earlier periods of US history, the NCLOE report turns to the question of crime and immigration in the 1930s. First the commission looked at the percentage of the population that is foreign born alongside the known offenses committed by this same population in a number of cities across the United States. It found that cities with high crime rates tended to be located at both ends of the scale in terms of percentage of foreign born; in other words, that there was no correlation between the two (NCLOE 1931, 93). Having more or fewer immigrants did not seem to have any relation to the crime rate of a given city, suggesting that local conditions unrelated to nativity were likely to blame.

While the foreign born generally often had been seen as predisposed to criminality, it was specific ethnic groups that were typically singled out, particularly in the latter nineteenth and early twentieth centuries. The commission looked at a number of cities in detail, with crime rates calculated not only for the foreign born generally but also for specific national groups. In the case of Los Angeles, it was found that Mexican nationals were far more likely than the native born to be arrested and convicted of felonies. Among the native born, 12.71 out of 10,000 were convicted of felonies, while for Mexicans the number was 54.85 (NCLOE 1931, 133). This finding would seem to suggest that the architects of S. 5094 had been right is citing the criminality of Mexican immigrants as a reason to attempt to deter undocumented immigration through criminal penalties and, in the case of reentrants, felony charges.

Because of anti-Mexican sentiment at the time and a propensity to characterize Mexican immigrants as criminal, an entire section of the NCLOE report is dedicated to a detailed examination of Mexican criminality. The findings seem to suggest that the high arrest and conviction rate for Mexican immigrants had little to do with any inherent criminality based on ethnicity. The first thing the report points out is that police officials commonly stated that Mexicans were more likely to plead guilty and to lack the funds for the "extended defense and appeal of cases" (NCLOE 1931, 204). This goes a long way toward explaining the high arrest and conviction rates for Mexican immigrants in Los Angeles. In some but not all cities examined in the report, the arrest rate for Mexicans was found to be disproportionate to their percentage of the population. A closer examination of these arrests revealed that many were owing to differences in culture between recent Mexican immigrants and Americans. Mexicans were more likely to carry weapons, usually knives, which resulted in arrest but was a common practice in Mexico according to testimonials quoted in the report (NCLOE 1931, 221). Another common reason for arrest was public drunkenness, which was illegal in the United States under Prohibition but was not in Mexico, nor was alcohol a prohibited substance there (NCLOE 1931, 221). Both suggest not any inherent criminality on the part of Mexican immigrants but instead the same difficulties in assimilation faced by any number of other groups. One person interviewed for the report in the Chicago-Gary region noted, "The Mexicans get a bad reputation through their drunkenness and court cases, which are played up by the papers and are the only things we hear about the Mexicans. Of course, the whites get drunk too" (NCLOE 1931, 223). The NCLOE found that the record when it came to Mexican criminality varied by location. In some cities, Mexicans were arrested and convicted at a higher rate than the native-born population, while in others the opposite was true. The report also notes that prejudice, poverty, language barriers, and aggressive actions on the part of law enforcement could have been the reasons behind the higher arrest and conviction rates in some cities. The section on Mexican immigrants concludes: "Is the Mexican really criminally inclined? Without hesitation, the conclusion is that he can not be consigned to such a category any more than any other nationality or race. . . . While numerous arrests and frequent convictions of Mexicans tend to make it appear that they are inclined to be delinquent, it is quite likely that such things rather point to misfortune, the lack of ingenuity and resources, and, in some instances, perhaps some discrimination against them" (NCLOE 1931, 328). The NCLOE thus found no support for Mexican criminality in its detailed examination of Mexican populations in a number of cities across the United States, suggesting that one of the premises on which S. 5094 was based was in fact a fallacy.

Like crime more broadly, Mexican criminality was determined by how local police and officials responded to Mexican immigrants, a lack of linguistic ability that would have allowed them to better understand the American legal system, poverty, and cultural practices brought with them from Mexico that led to conflicts with local police. With the passage of S. 5094, even if Mexican immigrants were not any more inclined to criminality than any other group, if they were undocumented they were criminals. S. 5094 would begin a long (and continuing) pattern of discussing Mexican immigrants in terms of their illegality and a rhetoric that painted them as criminals, if for no reason other than the way they entered the United States.

This tension between the reality and the politics of undocumented immigration is of course not unique to the early twentieth century. It reflects the constant contradiction in US immigration policy, in which discourses of threat are used to maintain control over a population necessary to the US economy. Mae Ngai uses the term *impossible subjects* to describe the undocumented in America because while they are, and have long been, a part of the social fabric of this country, they remain outside of it, foreigners in a country they helped to build. While the Irish, the Italians, and others were eventually accepted as Americans, Mexicans, and Latino immigrants more broadly, were not accepted because of their race. Even illegality was largely assigned to Mexican immigrants specifically, with undocumented European immigrants allowed to apply for "pre-examination" beginning in 1935. This allowed Europeans with a US-born spouse or child to be examined for legal admission to the United States and then to voluntarily depart to Canada, where they could go to the nearest consul and get their papers for permanent residence (Ngai 2004). While this means was technically available to undocumented Mexican immigrants, the distance to the Canadian border and their lack of understanding of how the process worked meant that few, if any, took advantage of it to normalize their status. In 1945, nationals of both Canada and Mexico were restricted from applying. Ngai points out that while this restriction was on its face race neutral since it excluded all countries that shared borders with the United States, it was specifically targeted at Mexican immigrants. "The racism of this policy was profound," writes Ngai, "for it denied, a priori, that deportation could cause hardship for the families of non-Europeans" (Ngai 2004, 87). Mexican immigrants were deemed both lesser and, on the heels of the passage of Johnson-Reed, more of a potential threat to American jobs, culture, and law and order than were European immigrants. Therefore, they were not offered the same opportunities for legalization as undocumented Europeans, ensuring that many Mexican immigrants would have to continue living in the shadows, fearing both deportation and criminal charges for illegal entry.

The passage of S. 5094 and the formal criminalization of undocumented reentry were followed by a campaign of "repatriation" that capitalized on the fears of Latino immigrants, both documented and undocumented, to drive them back to Mexico. High-profile raids and the announcement of these raids in immigrant neighborhoods led many to "voluntarily" repatriate, reducing the size of the Mexican population in the United States by hundreds of thousands (Balderrama 1995; Ngai 2004). This campaign of forced Mexican Repatriation by the INS ran from 1929, the year that the Undesirable Aliens Act was passed, to 1939, as the country struggled with the Depression and the increases in nativism that are a regular occurrence during economic downturns.

Not long after Mexican Repatriation ended, the United States was once again in need of Mexican laborers. To meet that need, in 1942 an agreement reached between President Manuel Avila Camacho of Mexico and President Franklin Roosevelt created the Bracero Program. The aim of the Bracero Program was to meet American labor demands while providing a solution to undocumented entry, which remained a normal occurrence despite the ten-year period of repatriation. The Bracero Program allowed Mexican workers to come to the United States as laborers under temporary contracts but also imposed minimal work conditions, wages, and employment protections for laborers (Ngai 2004; Tichenor 2002). These conditions in many cases made it easier for employers to simply return to the old arrangement with undocumented workers, since they faced no real penalties for hiring undocumented immigrants. Undocumented workers were targeted by the US government, though, with

Operation Wetback, whose stated goal was one thousand apprehensions a day, beginning in 1954 (Garcia 1980; Ngai 2004). Like the Bracero Program, Operation Wetback was a move by Mexican and American officials aimed at reducing the flow of undocumented immigrants through mass deportations and the threat of penalties for those captured. Operation Wetback would last until 1955, though deportations dropped significantly after 1954. The Bracero Program would continue until 1964 (Ngai 2004).

Yet there was no concrete congressional action on the problem of undocumented immigration. Congress largely ignored the issue of undocumented immigration, allowing the existing bureaucracies that had been set up to address it, the Border Patrol and the INS, to do their job, while relying on penalties for undocumented immigration that were part of S. 5094 to serve as a deterrent. The INS and the Border Patrol largely treated undocumented immigration as a crime-control issue through the threat of penalties and deportation, as well as neighborhood and workplace raids, under both Mexican Repatriation and Operation Wetback.

Unsurprisingly, apprehension, penalties, and deportation largely failed to reduce undocumented immigration, and in the early 1980s the American public increasingly saw it as an issue that needed to be addressed (Tichenor 2002). Additionally, the extension of national quotas to Mexico under the amendments to the Hart-Cellar Act in 1976 helped to exacerbate undocumented immigration, making it much more visible. A Gallup survey in 1984 asked participants whether they thought too many, too few, or about the right number of immigrants from different geographic areas were entering the country. Regarding European immigrants, only 26 percent of Americans believed that too many were entering the country, with 50 percent saying the number was about right. Regarding immigrants from Latin American countries, the result was almost the inverse, with 53 percent of Americans saying that too many were coming into the United States and 30 percent saying the number was about right (Gallup News 2016). Another poll found that 61 percent of Americans believed that immigrants were taking jobs away from Americans (Muller 1994). Immigration, especially undocumented immigration, was clearly seen as a problem by many Americans in the first half of the 1980s, and existing policy seemed to have done little to control it, forcing the Reagan administration to try to find a solution to a problem that had vexed the United States since the 1920s.

Rates of immigration soared in the 1980s, and undocumented immigration, though difficult to quantify exactly, increased as well. By 1980 the undocumented population was estimated to be 2–4 million, with roughly 1–2 million coming from Mexico (Warren and Passel 1987). This was a serious increase from the estimated 1,116,000 in 1974 (Tichenor 2002) (fig. A1). In addition to undocumented immigration, there were two other immigration-related crises in the first half of the 1980s. Wars and civil strife in Central America drove refugees to America's border, leading to the birth of the Sanctuary Movement in 1982. The Sanctuary Movement was a nationwide network of churches and synagogues that offered safe haven to undocumented immigrants from El Salvador and Guatemala who were fleeing violence but were frequently denied asylum in the United States. Because the United States was supporting the regimes responsible for the very violence these refugees were fleeing, they were routinely turned away as economic migrants (Ridgley 2008). The Mariel Boatlift from Cuba dropped an estimated 125,000 asylum seekers on the shores of Florida in 1980 (Tichenor 2002). The increasing rate of undocumented immigration and multiple crises attracted media attention, and with it the eyes of the American public (Stevens 2016; Tichenor 2002). A report by the Brooking Institution found that AP news coverage of immigration was higher in 1981 than in any year that followed, until 2000. Additionally, *New York Times* coverage in 1981 was higher than the average for the period 1980–2017 (Akdenizli et al. 2008). These figures highlight the amount of attention that undocumented immigration, the Mariel Boatlift and its aftermath, and the beginning of the Central American refugee crisis received in the American media, which influences public opinion (Zaller 1992).

The Reagan administration, which came to power in 1981, represented a strain of conservatism that "celebrated large-scale immigration and temporary worker programs" (Tichenor 2002). Reagan himself saw the solution to undocumented immigration as open borders as part of a free trade zone that would promote labor competition (Tichenor 2002). During the 1980 Republican primary debate between George H. W. Bush and Reagan, Reagan noted that Mexico had 40–50 percent unemployment. "Rather than talking about putting up a fence," suggested Reagan, "why don't we work out some recognition of our mutual problems, make it possible for them to come here legally with a work permit, and then while they're working and earning here, they pay taxes here. And then when they want to go back, they can go back and they can cross. And open the border both ways" (C-SPAN 1980). Undocumented immigration, while seen as problematic because of the way immigrants entered, was seen as necessary and a boon for the American economy by both

Reagan and Bush. Neither man felt that enforcement or criminalization would solve the problem of undocumented immigration. In the same debate, Bush stated, "We're creating a whole society of really honorable, decent, family-loving people that are in violation of the law" (C-SPAN 1980). This convergence of increasing public and media attention with an administration, and more broadly a Republican Party, that did not demonize Mexican immigrants but instead saw their contributions as important created a moment of punctuated equilibrium in immigration policy, which allowed for a shift in the solutions to undocumented immigration.

Baumgartner and Jones (1993) argue that policy agendas have a great deal of stability in American politics. In other words, shifts in how particular problems are both conceptualized and addressed through policy are rare and often occur at moments of punctuated equilibrium. Moments of punctuated equilibrium are often created by events or shifts in public opinion that open a window for a change in policy. In this case, the growing public attention to undocumented immigration owing to the numerous crises in the 1980s, as well as Reagan's personal views on undocumented immigration and its solutions, forced government officials to address the problem. The election of a president who saw undocumented immigration as a problem of supply and demand rather than one of criminality could lead to a shift in approach. While Reagan and Bush did emphasize that undocumented immigrants were good people, this was in some ways secondary to the economic argument, which viewed the labor of these immigrants as both necessary and beneficial to the economy of the United States.

The First Try: The Simpson-Mazzoli Bill

In 1982 a first attempt at a comprehensive solution to immigration through the Immigration Reform and Control Act of 1982 (also known as the Simpson-Mazzoli bill), which would have addressed not only undocumented immigration but also legal immigration, placing family members under the annual cap and limiting visas to brothers and sisters of citizens. This would have reduced immigration from Latin American countries, which had benefitted from the emphasis on family reunification that had been a hallmark of the Hart-Cellar Act of 1965, which did not count family members toward the total cap on immigration. The Hart-Cellar Act eliminated the national quotas system that had been put in place under Johnson-Reed, replacing it with hemispheric quotas and a cap of twenty thousand immigrants per country, though initially this was only applicable to the Eastern Hemisphere (Ngai 2004). The Western Hemisphere, including Mexico and Canada, would not become subject to quotas until 1976, and just two years later hemispheric quotas were eliminated entirely in favor of a worldwide limit (Tichenor 2002).

The Simpson-Mazzoli bill proposed employer sanctions for those employing undocumented immigrants to reduce undocumented immigration by eliminating (or weakening) one of the pull factors, the ease of employment (Tichenor 2002). It included amnesty and a guest-worker program, ingredients that would later become policy under IRCA; but it also was far broader, trying to address both legal and illegal immigration in one piece of legislation. The bill sailed through the Senate, largely owing to the Republican majority and the leadership of Senator Alan Simpson of Wyoming, who had been appointed to the Subcommittee on Immigration and Refugee Policy by Strom Thurmond of South Carolina, it failed in the Democratic-controlled House (Tichenor 2002). Amendment after amendment was met with resistance from a coalition of business interests and civil rights organizations, the latter concerned with the potential for discrimination because of employer sanctions and the elimination of the fifth preference category for visas to brothers and sisters of citizens. The Rules Committee in the House allowed an almost limitless number of amendments, with Democrat Edward Roybal of California proposing more than two hundred (Tichenor 2002).

The failure of Simpson-Mazzoli made one thing obvious: a comprehensive overhaul of both legal and undocumented immigration would be difficult, if not impossible. Therefore, the second Simpson-Mazzoli bill, which would become the Immigration Reform and Control Act of 1986, or the Simpson-Mazzoli Act, addressed only undocumented immigration. It was one of the first pieces of congressional legislation since the Undesirable Aliens Act of 1929 to specifically address undocumented immigration, the first to attempt to do so in a comprehensive fashion, and the first in US history to acknowledge the responsibility of both the immigrant and the employer.

While public perceptions of undocumented immigration were not necessarily sympathetic, the attention being paid to undocumented immigration meant that Congress and the Reagan administration were in search of a solution, and many acknowledged that compromise would be necessary. The decoupling of legal and illegal immigration in the final version of IRCA removed some of the resistance to the 1982 Simpson-Mazzoli bill, which had largely been to limiting visas to siblings of US citizens. Removing the question of legal immigration allowed the bill to be debated on the merits of its answers to undocumented immigration, which diverged from most policies on undocumented immigration that had been passed in the preceding fifty-seven years. If the new bill passed and was successful, it would represent a new path forward for tackling the problem of undocumented immigration, one that affirmed the humanity of the immigrants, while also seeking a solution that acknowledged the responsibility of both immigrants and employers.

While Reagan's rhetoric differed significantly from what had been typical in the debate over undocumented immigration, it is not clear that the same was true for Congress, which would be responsible for passing the legislation. While the opinion of the president matters for legislation and can play a role in its passage or failure, ultimately the fate of the revised Simpson-Mazzoli bill would lie with the House and the Senate. Would congressional rhetoric be softened as much as presidential rhetoric had been?

The congressional debate on IRCA offers insight into broader elite perceptions of undocumented immigration and the shift that occurred in terms of the criminality frame, and threat frames more generally, in the 1980s, as a number of events created a moment of punctuated equilibrium, opening the door to a major overhaul of US policy on undocumented immigration for the first time since the 1920s. At the same time, the expectations for IRCA made it critical for the future of immigration legislation, with any failures likely to engender a reentrenchment of immigration restriction and criminal penalties.

The Immigration Reform and Control Act of 1986

The debate over IRCA was very different from the earlier debates on undocumented immigration. Unlike the Johnson-Reed and S. 5094 debates, the debate on IRCA focused largely on the nuts and bolts of implementation. The bill was the result of compromise and thus not an ideal piece of legislation for most, but it was what was possible given the divided Congress, public opinion on undocumented immigration, and the need for action. In the House debate, Representative Roybal of California pointed out that "many have said that they would vote for the bill, but with mixed emotions. Others said that they would hold their nose to vote for this piece of legislation. Others just would vote for the bill simply because there was nothing else" (132nd Cong. Rec., 30067). Although not everyone was happy with the bill, it was seen as a necessity, because immigration reform was seen as a necessity. "We are at a time of crisis in the enforcement of our immigration laws," said Republican

Hamilton Fish of New York. "The public perception that immigration is out of control is, unfortunately, a correct perception" (132nd Cong. Rec., 29987). Fish went beyond simply suggesting that the current public opinion on immigration made action necessary. If nothing was done, in Fish's view, it was very likely that a future Congress would return to restrictionism as a solution. "If we fail to enact reform in this Congress, I fear that when a later Congress considers immigration reform, it will produce a bill which will be narrow and restrictive. It will be driven toward passage by the pent-up frustration of the American people" (132nd Cong. Rec., 29987). Fish was expressing the opinion, undoubtedly shared by many, that IRCA represented a unique opportunity to overhaul undocumented immigration in a way that was not driven by nativism or a reaction to the anger of the public, but instead by bipartisanship and an acknowledgment of the realities of labor demands.

The need for workers and its role in drawing undocumented immigrants were acknowledged repeatedly in the debate over IRCA. In the Senate, Republican Pete Wilson of California echoed the sentiments of many when he argued, "Nothing is going to change the need for these workers, who are willing to risk a great deal to come in, in the dead of night, fearing danger . . . in order to work. Now, is it right or is it fair, Mr. President, that these people, who are simply seeking to earn an honest living, should be compelled to do so illegally?" (132nd Cong. Rec., 24086). Similar sentiments were voiced throughout the debate in both the House and the Senate, representing a notable contrast to the way Mexican and undocumented immigration had been discussed during debate on Johnson-Reed and S. 5094.

Framing Undocumented Immigration: IRCA in the House

Debate in the House, where Democrats held a 253–182 majority, was much more contentious than debate in the Senate, which focused mainly on fine-tuning the bill via amendments and questions about implementation. Overall, I coded approximately 48 pages of the Congressional Record coded for House debate on IRCA. In these 48 pages, there were almost as many references to threat frames as in the roughly 118 pages I coded for the Senate debate. There were thirty-one unique mentions of phrases tied to the criminal threat frame during the House debate, though many of these were uses of the terms *illegal alien, illegal immigrant,* and *illegal* to describe the target group for the legislation. Because approximately 66 percent of the American public agree with the statement "Crossing the border illegally is a crime and immigrants who come

TABLE 2.1. Threat frames in the Congressional IRCA debate: Unique mentions / number of congresspersons mentioning

FRAME	SENATE	HOUSE
Positive economic	7/5	6/5
Negative economic	10/6	10/10
Positive cultural	1/1	1/1
Negative cultural	2/2	1/1
Positive criminal	3/2	2/2
Negative criminal (including *illegal*)	28/16	31/27
Negative criminal (excluding *illegal*)	2/1	10/10

to the US this way are criminals," I coded references to the immigrants themselves as illegals or illegal immigrants or aliens as 1 for the criminal threat frame, but for IRCA I coded for the criminal threat frame references both with and without the term *illegal.* In addition, since IRCA was almost exclusively concerned with Mexican immigration, I did no coding for nationality. Table 2.1 shows a breakdown for the various threat frames and the number of senators and representatives mentioning those frames.

As table 2.1 reveals, there were 31 mentions of the criminal threat frame including the term *illegal* by 27 representatives, giving this frame the highest overall number of unique mentions, was followed by the economic threat frame, with 10 unique mentions. Removing just use of the word *illegal* to describe undocumented immigrants still left 10 unique mentions in the House, tying it with the economic threat frame. Republican Ron Packard of California gave one of the more lurid descriptions of the crimes committed by undocumented immigrants: "In my district . . . we have a tragic increase in drugs, crime, prostitution, and social problems. Now I read in the San Diego Union that the aliens are preying upon our schoolchildren and stealing their lunch money" (132nd Cong. Rec., 30008). Democrat Buddy MacKay of Florida later made a similar statement on the House floor during debate over an amendment that would have expedited deportation hearings for undocumented immigrants found guilty of drug-related offenses and transferred them into the federal system to facilitate faster deportation. He noted that "63 percent of the narcotics arrests in southern California are illegal immigrants. These are people going into a system that is already overfilled, they are being released; they are committing further crimes and we have a revolving door effect there" (132nd Cong. Rec., 30069). Representative Smith of Florida joined his fellow Democrat in pushing for the amendment, voicing his concern that "as more and more illegal aliens get into the business of drug trafficking and get into the other business of crime, more and more States are going to be impacted by the problems that have occurred now" (132nd Cong. Rec., 30069). Both statements harken back to earlier statements about the potential violence of undocumented immigrants and the perception of criminality beyond just their status as "illegals." Representative Dante Fascell, a fellow Democrat from Florida, echoed these concerns, arguing that undocumented immigrants were involved in drug trafficking and crime and that states were receiving little assistance from the federal government to deal with this problem (132nd Cong. Rec., 30069–70).

Some of the resistance to IRCA in the House was driven by a perception that the amnesty program rewarded criminal behavior with legalization. Representative Barton of Texas argued, "If we condone amnesty, we are condoning an illegal act of those illegal immigrants who have entered this country illegally" (132nd Cong. Rec., 30064). This sentiment was echoed by Republican Bill McCollum of Florida, who very similarly pointed out that "we are going to be rewarding lawbreakers; people who have been here illegally who have no business becoming citizens and permanent residents" (132nd Cong. Rec., 30063). This perception that undocumented immigrants were being rewarded through amnesty was also drawn on to highlight the fact that legal immigrants still had to go through a long process to achieve what undocumented immigrants were getting by simply crossing the border and avoiding deportation. The criminality frame in the House, then, revolved around notions that undocumented immigrants were involved with criminal activity and that at the very least amnesty would function as a reward for past illegal behavior.

In the House debate, as noted in table 2.1, concerns were also expressed about the economic threat undocumented immigrants posed. Republican Jack Fields of Texas noted that "I am a native of and represent a southern border state—Texas, I am well aware of the problems associated with illegal immigration: The costs to public hospitals, the costs for public health services, the increase in criminal activity and job displacement" (132nd Cong. Rec., 30004). This was a slightly different economic concern than in the debate over Johnson-Reed or S. 5094, which tended to be focused solely on labor and the notion that undocumented immigrants took jobs from Americans. The Republican William Dannemeyer of California similarly spoke of the economic threat associated with undocumented immigration: "Though San Diego County has endured countless hardships in the course of the struggle with illegal immigration, Los Angeles County has not escaped its share of economic and social devastation." He gave $200 million as the supposed cost to the taxpayers of Los Angeles County of providing health, justice, and social services to the undocumented community. Representative Dannemeyer noted the burden imposed by birthright citizenship and the fact that the illegal mothers of children born on US soil could claim welfare benefits, costing county taxpayers an estimated $8 million per month (132nd Cong. Rec., 30005). Overall, then, the economic threat frame differed in the case of IRCA, with more of a focus on the burden of undocumented immigration, emphasizing the cost to taxpayers of providing social services to those who were (and are) characterized as not paying taxes. A 2005 *New York Times* article by Eduardo Porter notes that while undocumented immigration is often characterized as a burden on taxpayers, it can be a boon to Social Security, since immigrants pay in but can never collect. "IRCA, as the immigration act is known, did little to deter employers from hiring illegal immigrants or to discourage them from working. But for Social Security's finances it was a great piece of legislation" (Porter 2005). The characterization of undocumented workers in terms of the cost they impose, during the IRCA debate and in other instances, is thus much more complicated than it is usually acknowledged to be

Some also specifically cited the potential costs of amnesty itself. Republican Hal Daub of Nebraska argued that amnesty would place a severe strain on state and local governments. He claimed that it would result in soaring welfare claims and a burden on the educational system as more undocumented children began attending school since their parents no longer had to fear deportation (132nd Cong. Rec., 30003). Undocumented children had been found to have a constitutional right to a K–12 education in *Plyler v. Doe* in 1982. This fear that amnesty would lead to former undocumented immigrants becoming an even greater burden on the state was another justification for opposing IRCA, or more specifically its amnesty proposal, though of course the alternative was to leave millions of people already in the United States without status, about which some expressed concerns. These concerns were not necessarily tied to a desire to treat the immigrants themselves in a more humane way, but to concerns raised by the economic threat frame. Representative Smith of Florida drew on the economic threat frame to justify amnesty, attesting, "What is something that you will very rarely be told is the truth about what it is costing America by having all these illegal aliens here not paying taxes, drawing Federal services, drawing state and local services which the taxpayers of America are paying for. . . . By making these people come forward out of the shadows, out of that subrosa economy, we are going to help the United States" (132nd Cong. Rec., 29991). While the criminal and economic threat frames were present in the House debate, there were far fewer references to the cultural threat in the House, with only Representative Dannemeyer's statement about the social "devastation" resulting from undocumented immigration coded as denoting a cultural threat. A number of positive comments were made on behalf of undocumented immigrants, the most common being about their economic contribution. For example, Democrat Henry Gonzalez of Texas countered claims of their being an economic burden by saying, "The fact is, that with respect to taxation, work and productivity, many of these undocumented workers are contributing a great deal in a great many places" (132nd Cong. Rec., 29993). Representative Gonzalez drew on the president's own economic report, which stated that "the presence of these aliens is beneficial economically to the United States" (132nd Cong. Rec., 29992). As table 2.1 shows, five members of the House specifically mentioned the economic contributions made by undocumented immigrants during debate over IRCA. The immigrants themselves were also positively characterized by some, such as Representative Dan Lungren of California, who argued that while many Americans were against undocumented immigration, many Americans also would make exceptions for specific individuals. "That is not schizophrenia," he said; "I think it is a recognition that most of the illegal aliens who are here are good people. They are humane people, they have come here to work, and when we know them, we in most cases like them and we will go out for them" (132nd Cong. Rec., 29986). Some also took issue with the characterization of undocumented immigrants as criminals. Representative Bill Richardson of New Mexico pushed back on both the economic and criminal threat frames, stating that IRCA would "allow 5, 7, 8, 9 million people to come out of bondage, people who are not criminals, as some of my colleagues have said, but have been contributing to society, have been taking jobs that we do not want" (132nd Cong. Rec., 30064). These positive characterizations of undocumented immigrants had been almost entirely lacking from the debate over S. 5094. Even when the law-abiding nature of undocumented immigrants was not explicitly noted, it was implied.

There was an interesting division in terminology in the House, with some individuals using the term *undocumented* and others using *illegal* to describe Mexican immigrants. This suggests that there was at least some acknowledgment by the 1980s that *illegal* was a loaded term, carrying connotations of criminality, and that *undocumented* carried less negative symbolism. The use of the term *undocumented* instead of *illegal* is also indicative of IRCA's more liberal approach to immigration policy and perhaps a recognition that a "rebranding" of undocumented immigration was in some ways necessary to ease passage of the bill. That said, in some cases the terms *illegal* and *undocumented* were used interchangeably by those who generally made positive statements about undocumented immigrants. It is unclear whether the use of one term over the other had any effect on members of the House who perhaps were on the fence regarding the bill or on public opinion. Drawing on a series of survey experiments, Merolla, Ramakrishnan, and Haynes (2013) found that the use of *undocumented* rather than *illegal* had little effect on public opinion on immigration policy. It is of course unclear whether these same effects would have been found in the 1980s or whether the public was the target of the shift in terminology during congressional debate on IRCA.

In the House, eliminating the use of *illegal* from the criminality frame resulted in exactly twenty-one unique negative framings of undocumented immigration. There were nine positive framings. Thus, the House debate on IRCA, when not specifically concerned with the logistics of implementation or concerns about specific parts of the bill, was for the most part negative in its portrayal of undocumented population, with more negative framings than positive framings, and by a larger number of representatives, at least in how the immigrants themselves were characterized. Criminality, intertwined with notions of illegality as it had been in 1929 in the debate over S. 5094, remained a common trope in the House debate over IRCA. Even so, the discourse in the House was much less charged than had been expected. While there were a number of mentions of the threats posed by undocumented immigration, even many of the individuals citing these concerns also professed a support for immigration reform, though they typically also wanted changes to be made to IRCA and a greater emphasis on border security. The Senate debate over IRCA in the Senate shared some similarities with that in the House but also differed in important ways in relation to the criminality frame.

Framing Undocumented Immigration: IRCA in the Senate

Debate on IRCA in the Senate mirrored the debate in the House in many ways, though there was much more debate overall in the Senate. Much of the Senate debate concerned amendments and implementation, particularly the possibility that employer sanctions could lead to discrimination against those who looked like they could be undocumented immigrants, such as American-born Latinos. Like the House debate, the Senate debate was almost entirely about Mexican immigration.

Table 2.1 shows a notable difference between the House and Senate characterizations of undocumented immigration regarding criminality. When the term *illegal* was included in the criminality frame, there were 28 mentions of the criminality frame in the Senate by 16 senators, which is similar to the 31 mentions in the House, though the Senate debate was much longer. However, when the term *illegal* was removed from the coded responses, there were only 2 mentions of the criminality frame by just 1 senator. This is significantly lower than the 10 in the House, making criminality a distant second to the economic threat frame, which was brought up 10 times by 6 different senators. However, even the economic framing was relatively balanced, with 7 positive economic framings by 5 senators over the course of the IRCA debate. The positive framing of undocumented immigration in the Senate largely focused on the economic contributions made by immigrants, as it had in the House debate. As in the House, the cultural threat frame was rarely mentioned in the Senate.

Republican senator Alfonse D'Amato of New York was responsible for both criminal threat framings in the Senate debate. In both cases, he emphasized the burden that was placed on state and local governments in dealing with criminal immigrants and pushed for reimbursement of the cost of incarcerating these individuals. In one statement, Senator D'Amato argued that "more than 3,000 illegal aliens and more than 1,700 Marielito Cuban felons released from Castro's prisons in 1980, have been convicted of felonies and are now adding to the overcrowding in our state prisons" (132nd Cong. Rec., 23832). In his other statement the senator noted that undocumented immigrants were clogging the prison system at a cost to taxpayers. While D'Amato's comments were directed at least in part at Mexicans, Senator Steve Symms, a Republican from Idaho, did mention fears that Nicaraguan terrorists could use the porousness of the southern US border as a way of entering the country to commit terrorist activities and that "dangerous drugs of all kinds" were being smuggled in from Cuba and Mexico (132nd Cong. Rec., 23808). This statement was not counted toward the criminality frame, as it was not directed at undocumented Mexican immigrants, which is the primary focus of this book.

In the more than one hundred pages of Senate debate coded, Senator D'Amato was the only individual to frame undocumented Mexican immigration in terms of criminality. This contrasts sharply with framing in the House, where there were more mentions of the criminal threat frame and more individuals referencing this frame in opposition to IRCA. In the Senate, the economic threat frame was the frame most commonly referenced in opposition to IRCA or as a reason to amend parts of the bill. Republican Paula Hawkins of Florida cited the potential outrage on the part of the public if "they knew how easy it is for illegal aliens to get benefits, aid for dependent children, unemployment compensation, Medicaid, and food stamps, at a time when we are . . . trying to come within the budget, trying to cut a million here and a million there" (132nd Cong. Rec., 23711). Democrat Ted Kennedy of Massachusetts referenced the threat posed by "the flood of migrants coming to this country" to take the jobs of American workers if an amendment offered by Pete Wilson of California were to pass (132nd Cong. Rec., 24086). This threat to the American worker was referenced frequently in debate over Wilson's amendment in the Senate, which would have set up a guest-worker program that initially contained no explicit cap on the number of guest workers who could be brought in. The Wilson amendment would fail by two votes in the Senate, but it was revived with a cap of 350,000 and managed to squeak by. Wilson's guest-worker program was replaced in the final version of IRCA with the Seasonal Agricultural Worker (SAW) and Replacement Agricultural Worker (RAW) programs (Baker 1990). While concerns with a guest-worker program certainly accounted for most the content in the ten economic threat frames, there were, as mentioned above, concerns about the burden on social services and the justice system. Senator James McClure of Idaho raised another concern that had to do with deportation itself. During debate, in response to Senator Simpson's statement that most apprehended undocumented immigrants were not deported but instead departed voluntarily, McClure cited the economic burden imposed by these departures on taxpayers, saying, "I understand a good many of them wait until the end of the season and turn themselves in so they can get their way home paid by the taxpayers of the United States" (132nd Cong. Rec., 23597). The statements about the economic threat in the Senate were much more moderate in tone than those of the House.

The number of positive frames in the Senate debate was similar to the number in the House debate, with the positive economic frame being the most common and the criminal and cultural frames at the lower end. There were two positive criminal framings as well as two positive cultural framings. One of the most impassioned positive statements came from Senator Ted Kennedy: "We are attempting, with this proposal [legalization of status for undocumented immigrants who had been in the United States for five years], to make those individuals who have demonstrated from their past conduct a commitment to this country, a commitment to society, a commitment to their family and their community, and to insure there will not be a constant sense of fear and to be able to . . . adjust their status and move toward citizenship" (132nd Cong. Rec., 23724). This cultural framing focused on the positive attributes of undocumented immigrants in a way that was meant to challenge longstanding perceptions of this group as a cultural threat to the United States by acknowledging their work ethic and their dedication to their families. The two references coded for the positive criminal frame both mentioned that undocumented immigrants were honest workers despite the situation they found themselves in.

Kennedy's positive cultural framing is interesting in light of his later comments that undocumented workers represented a threat to American workers, though in that instance he was speaking specifically of the Wilson amendment and the admission of what he believed were far too many immigrants when there was substantial unemployment in the United States. Senator Kennedy's position on the cultural and economic threats posed by the undocumented highlights the inherent difficulties in trying to normalize the status of the millions while implementing a guest-worker program to reduce future undocumented immigrations. Believing that undocumented immigrants are, for the most part, good people does not mean that you cannot also see them as a potential threat to American jobs.

Indeed, one of the most interesting aspects of the debate on IRCA was how often it was mentioned that not only the immigrants themselves but their employers and the US government were responsible for undocumented immigration, the former for crossing the border illegally, the latter for allowing a system to remain in place that both incentivized and encouraged undocumented immigration to meet labor demands. Republican Steve Symms of Idaho stressed that "out there in the real world, where the produce is being harvested, there is an illegal guest worker program in place right now. It is happening whether we like to think about it in the Senate or not" (132nd Cong. Rec., 23592). Senator Kennedy pointed out the hypocrisy of placing responsibility solely on the immigrant, professing that " it is wrong that the sanctions under current law fall solely on the undocumented aliens, not on employers who may be exploiting them" (132nd Cong. Rec., 23320). Senator Hawkins explicitly noted the pull factor in employment and the potential employer sanction had to reduce undocumented immigration by reducing or eliminating the "lure that draws illegals here in the first place" (132nd Cong. Rec., 23709). These comments represent an interesting about-face in terms of how the undocumented-immigration problem was conceptualized between S. 5094 and IRCA fifty-seven years later. In the debate on S. 5094, while labor demands were acknowledged, nearly all the responsibility for undocumented immigration was placed on the immigrant, who was seen as flouting US immigration law by entering the country illegally. This narrative of criminality favors deterrence through punishment, which has been US policy for most of the history of undocumented immigration. IRCA represented not only a novel approach to the problem of undocumented immigration but also a shift in opinion about the causes of undocumented immigration. In the IRCA debate it was acknowledged that the immigrant, the employer, and the US government all had contributed to the problem and that a comprehensive solution was required. This recognition and probably also the fact that simply penalizing the immigrants themselves had done little to reduce undocumented immigration led IRCA to expand criminalization to also include the employer.

On the side of a positive economic framing of undocumented immigration, a number of statements were similar to those cited above. In most, the necessity of immigrant labor was noted, and in some the difficulty of the labor was mentioned. Pete Wilson argued for the economic benefits of undocumented immigration: "Men and women who are willing to work, and work hard, in the sun and in the weather, will at least have the peace of mind to know that their hard work will not be interrupted by a raid, that there will be no swooping down upon them in the fields, that they will not be compelled to live in holes, like animals. This is a situation we should not tolerate in the United States" (132nd Cong. Rec., 23838). Democrat Dennis DeConcini of Arizona argued that in regard to the harvesting of perishable crops, undocumented immigrants were "the only workers willing, able, and available to do this vital work" (132nd Cong. Rec., 23584). Similar positive statements were made regarding the economic value and necessity of immigrant labor.

Thus, IRCA differed significantly from either Johnson-Reed or S. 5094 in terms of how Mexican immigration, and especially undocumented immigration, was framed. While statements were made regarding the threat posed by undocumented immigrants, the focus was on the actual difficulties of addressing undocumented immigration as a policy issue rather than on the immigrants themselves. In addition, there were few references to the cultural threat posed by undocumented immigrants, with most threat frames being economic in nature. Concerns about immigrant criminality, at least in the House, were second only to concerns about the economic burden the immigrants would be or the threat they posed to American labor. Between the House and the Senate, there were fourteen negative criminal framings for Johnson-Reed and twelve for IRCA. Most of the mentions of criminality in the IRCA debate were regarding criminal immigrants, not illegals more broadly as in the debate on S. 5094. Aside from a few individuals, most members of Congress, when discussing the criminality of undocumented immigrants, tended to limit their comments to specific subsets of the undocumented.

Analyzing the policy narratives in the congressional debate over IRCA, Lina Newton found that two rhetorical frames were associated with undocumented immigrants. The first was what she calls the "undeserving illegal" narrative, which focused on themes like the ones I touched on above. This policy frame constructed undocumented immigrants as lawbreakers, as a flood that would overwhelm American labor, and as undeserving of citizenship (Newton 2008, 98). However, unlike in previous debates, this narrative was met by a counternarrative of the "deserving illegal," which constructed undocumented immigrants as law-abiding, family-oriented, valuable members of their community and as future taxpayers and American citizens. Newton also cites another five policy narratives that were mentioned in the IRCA debate. Most of these narratives targeted employers and agricultural interests, while one very specifically targeted minority and foreign-born job applicants. The narratives reflect the complexity of the IRCA debate and how it differed from the earlier debates, which at best noted the economic necessity of Mexican immigrants, though often while demonizing them.

As mentioned earlier, this shift in rhetoric was the result of an acknowledgment that undocumented immigration was necessary and that dealing with the continuing issue of undocumented entry required a comprehensive response that also addressed US labor demands. The necessity of comprehensive reform was acknowledged regularly in the IRCA debate, with Representative Lungren stating that "elements that make up an immigration reform bill must be crafted to work with one another" (132nd Cong. Rec., 29986). Amnesty, the SAW and RAW programs, and employer sanctions, coupled with increased immigration enforcement by the Border Patrol and the INS, would, it was believed, lead to a substantial reduction in undocumented immigration. The convergence of multiple events made IRCA possible by creating a moment of punctuated equilibrium in immigration policy that allowed a break from the path dependence of the criminality regime that had long dominated the policy arena when it came to undocumented immigration. A divided Congress, the Reagan administration's recognition of the need for immigrant labor, and the growing public and media pressure on the federal government all helped make possible a change in US immigration policy and a move away from treating undocumented immigration simply as an issue of crime control. In addition, IRCA separated legal and illegal immigration, allowing for a true debate on the causes and solutions to undocumented immigration for the first time in US history. In the past, undocumented immigration had rarely been discussed on its own, instead being combined with issues relating to legal immigration and making any comprehensive solution difficult. While threat frames were still common, the debate over IRCA was surprisingly balanced compared with the earlier debates.

Criminalization and IRCA

IRCA ultimately passed in both the House and the Senate and was signed into law by President Reagan on November 6, 1986. In its final form, it extended amnesty to those who had been in the United States continuously since January 1, 1982, as well as certain seasonal workers under the SAW program. The SAW program was in many ways a more palatable guest-worker program, allowing employers to continue to use their current labor force and allowing those working in agriculture to normalize their status. SAW was driven by concerns with the size of a guest-worker program such as the one suggested by Pete Wilson of California, which could have admitted up to 350,000 workers at any one time, while the Reagan administration had favored admitting 50,000 annually (Baker 1990; Immigration Reform and Control Act of 1986). SAW required that Group 1 applicants prove that they had worked in agriculture for ninety days in each of the twelve-month periods between May 1, 1984, and May 1, 1986. They also had to have resided in the United States for at six months of each twelve-month period before they could normalize their status. Group 2 SAWs had to have worked for ninety days in the twelve-month period ending on May 1, 1986. In addition, the RAW program allowed more agricultural workers to be brought in when the Departments of Agriculture and Labor determined that there was a need for more workers. Immigrants would have to work in agriculture ninety days over the next three years to avoid deportation and be eligible for permanent residence (Immigration Reform and Control Act of 1986).

Criminalization was not absent from IRCA. One of the legs of the "three-legged stool" upon which IRCA was based was increased enforcement of existing immigration laws and border control. IRCA included criminal penalties for the use of fraudulent documents and for knowingly transporting, harboring, or bringing undocumented immigrants into the United States (Chishti, Meissner, and Bergeron 2011). While undocumented immigrants were framed in a more positive light in the IRCA debate, a distinction must be drawn between its effect on those immigrants already inside the United States and its effect on those who had yet to enter. Criminalization was directed at new entrants, who could not benefit from the amnesty or the SAW program because both required that the individual had been residing in the United States for a period prior to application. Employer sanctions were introduced to deter the hiring of undocumented workers and could carry criminal penalties for repeated violations. These sanctions were a crucial part of IRCA because requiring employers to verify that their employees could legally work in the United States would remove the pull factor of jobs. According to Senator McCollum, "The guts of this legislation, the critical point behind it all, is that in order to control our borders, we simply have to make it illegal for an employer to knowingly hire an illegal alien" (132nd Cong. Rec., 29990). It must be noted that employer penalties were referred to as "sanctions" throughout the debate on IRCA and were not criminal penalties. They were essentially intended to incentivize verifying eligibility by threatening fines for failing to do so. To be charged with a crime, employers had to show a "pattern or practice of violations" of the verification requirement.

Despite the continued reliance on criminalization for deterrence, IRCA, as the first piece of legislation to try to comprehensively address undocumented immigration, marked a shift in both the framing during congressional debate and the approach taken to address the issue. The importance of IRCA's approach to undocumented immigration cannot be overstated. It created an amnesty program for millions of undocumented immigrants in the United States; through the SAW and RAW programs it created the first guest-worker program since the end of the Bracero Program in 1942; and it penalized the employers of undocumented immigrants, who for so long had faced no consequences. While it also increased border and interior enforcement, this was no longer the sole focus of congressional policy. Attempts at similar comprehensive immigration reform failed under both the George W. Bush and Barack Obama administrations in part because of the difficulties in managing competing interests in such a broad bill.

While there was a shift in how the United States approached the problem of undocumented immigration under IRCA, a failure on the part of the guest-worker and employer-penalty programs made a return to criminalization as a solution likely; the path most traveled would become, once again, the most appealing, as it would entail lower political costs and had been the norm for the period preceding IRCA. Criminalization is, at the end of day, one of the less politically risky solutions, since it calls to mind fences, more Border Patrol officers, more INS agents, more detention facilities, all of which create an image of safety even if they do little to address the causes of undocumented immigration. As in the case of crime control, the politically safe solution fails to adequately address the actual causes. An approach that tackles the problems of poverty, poor education, addiction, and rehabilitation takes longer to produce measurable outcomes and is therefore a harder sell. The criminalization of immigration that preceded IRCA was never truly rolled back, and it would be reinforced in the post-IRCA period because of its measurable short-term outcomes: more deportations by ICE, new detention facilities, and, as was suggested by Donald Trump, "a great border wall" (Trump 2016b).

When IRCA was passed, it had the potential to be a critical policy failure if the flow of undocumented immigration failed to be reduced because of the massive shift it attempted in terms of problem framing and policy. With limited policy approaches available and with IRCA's shortcomings undermining liberal approaches, the likelihood was that the United States would return to an immigration approach based almost solely on criminalization and border militarization. Unfortunately, this came to pass, as many key provisions of the bill would fail to slow undocumented immigration, which was particularly damning in the case of amnesty.

As stated above, the amnesty program set up under IRCA applied to those who had been in the United States since January 1, 1982, as well as to certain agricultural workers, and resulted in the legalization of an estimated 2.7 million formerly undocumented immigrants (Chishti and Kamasaki 2014). While the amnesty program was a success, the other provisions of IRCA ultimately came up short. The employer sanctions contained enough loopholes that the reliance on undocumented labor was never appreciably reduced. Employers who obtained undocumented workers through a third party faced no consequences if those workers had fraudulent documents, as they were not required to verify their authenticity (Chishti and Kamasaki 2014; Tichenor 2002). The INS was responsible for oversight of employer sanctions but could not adequately enforce them, and there was a boom in the fraudulent documents industry after IRCA's passage (Chishti, Meissner, and Bergeron 2011). The SAW and RAW programs did not allow enough immigrants to come in nor streamline the process enough to make the guest-worker program set up by IRCA a viable solution. Concerns about the revival of something similar to the Bracero Program, which many in the 1980s had seen as undesirable, led to a one-time legalization program for seasonal workers (SAW) and a replenishment program (RAW) to address future needs. However, the RAW program would only have allowed more to enter pending an assessment of need by two different departments, which didn't allow for a great deal of flexibility. No laborers were actually admitted under the RAW program, as the assessment found no need for additional labor (Baker 1990). Because of this, as well as the loopholes in employer sanctions, farmers and agricultural interests instead returned to their reliance on undocumented labor, and the size of the undocumented population once again began to increase (Tichenor 2002).

Lastly, the increase in the size of the Border Patrol and the increased militarization of the border limited the ability of undocumented immigrants to move back and forth between the United States and Mexico, which had been much more common in the period preceding IRCA. Douglas Massey and Audrey Singer (1995) estimated that between 1965 and 1985 up to 85 percent of undocumented entries were offset by immigrants returning to Mexico, which was severely hampered by IRCA's expansion of the Border Patrol. If undocumented immigrants feared that they would not be able to return to the United States for the seasonal labor that in many cases provided for their families, they were less likely to leave. This helped to drastically increase the number of undocumented immigrants residing in the United States on a largely permanent basis, which made IRCA look like even more of a failure as the undocumented population grew throughout the 1990s (Massey 2007).

Because of the growing undocumented population, undocumented immigration was once again seen as a problem, and the public once again demanded action. Following passage of IRCA, the estimated size of the undocumented population dropped from 3.2 million in 1986 to 1.9 million in 1988, but by 1990 it had risen to 3.5 million (Wasem 2012). IRCA had clearly failed to reduce the flow of undocumented immigration, with the increase in 1990 larger than the decrease between 1986 and 1988. The amnesty program now appeared to have legalized undocumented immigrants for no reason, and employer sanctions had clearly failed to dissuade hiring because of the loopholes exploited by US employers. The result was a critical policy failure that would, in turn, lead to legislation that returned to criminalization as the primary means of addressing undocumented immigration, the Illegal Immigration Reform and Immigrant Responsibility Act of 1996. This result had been predicted by Representative Hamilton Fish of New York, who had stressed that IRCA was important because the failure to act could result in a return to restrictionism (132nd Cong. Rec., 29987). Unfortunately, it was instead the failure of IRCA to reduce undocumented immigration that led to the very shift Fish had warned of. IIRIRA was a repudiation of the more balanced approach attempted under IRCA and a return to a policy of criminalization, which once again laid responsibility solely on the immigrant. By 1996 there were an estimated five million undocumented immigrants in the United States despite the extension of permanent residency to approximately 2.7 million undocumented immigrants under IRCA (Cooper and O'Neil 2005; Pew Research Hispanic Trends Project 2013).

The Illegal Immigration Reform and Immigrant Responsibility Act of 1996

As Bill Clinton entered the White House in 1992, crime and undocumented immigration were both issues of public concern, with several events putting immigration control was front and center in American politics. According to Dawn Johnson (2001), the first of these events was the heated debate over California's Proposition 187 in 1994, which sought to deny schooling to the children of undocumented immigrants and called attention to the number of undocumented immigrants in the California school system. Pete Wilson, who had been a staunch supporter of IRCA, also led the push for Proposition 187, in a shift that presaged the IIRIRA debate in 1996. The rhetoric around Proposition 187, which would have prevented undocumented immigrants from accessing public education or nonemergency health care services, focused heavily on narratives of criminality (R. D. Jacobson 2008). Johnson also cites the passage of the North American Free Trade Agreement in 1994 as focusing the public's attention on immigration and its impact on the US economy. Finally, the 1993 bombing of the World Trade Center by someone identified as an immigrant heightened the public's perception of immigration as a potential terrorist threat (Johnson 2001). Concern about crime was also at a historic high in 1994, a fact seized upon early by the Clinton administration (Alexander 2010). Many political elites saw a link between crime and undocumented immigration, a linkage that has long been a concern in regard to narcotics trafficking.

To these concerns about crime and terrorism must also be added the nativism that motivated support for Proposition 187, according to Robin Dale Jacobson (2008). This nativism was likely driven, at least in part, by Census projections that saw the white population shrinking from a three-quarter share to just about 50 percent. An article in the *Washington Post* on December 4, 1992, noted that the Hispanic population was set to quadruple by 2050, when it would constitute more than a fifth of the US population (Vobejda 1992). For those concerned about the declining white population the news did not get better. An article on the front page of the *New York Times* on August 29, 1995, noted that a recent report by the US Census had placed the percentage of the country's foreign-born population at its highest since World War II (Holmes 1995). The new Census report also noted a declining birthrate among native-born Americans, while the birthrate among immigrants remained high. This raised the specter of an America where whites were in the minority and triggered nativist reactions from right-wing writers such as Peter Brimelow, whose *Alien Nation: Common Sense about America's Immigration Disaster*, published in 1995, would be a bestseller, reflecting the salience of the debate around immigration in the 1990s. Brimelow charged that the 1965 Hart-Cellar Act, in dispensing with national quotas and privileging family reunification, had increased immigration from developing nations, which presented a number of problems for the United States. Brimelow argued that the work force entering America since 1965 had been larger and less skilled than when immigration policy had favored European immigrants, that this work force was "probably not beneficial economically," that it would bring about a "ethnic and racial transformation in America," and that it had a number of additional negative consequences ranging from the "physical environment" to the political (Brimelow 1995, 9). One of these negative consequences was, somewhat predictably, crime. Citing the crime epidemic in the United States (which itself was questionable at the time), Brimelow histrionically noted, "Yet almost no Americans are aware *that aliens make up one quarter of the prisoners in federal penitentiaries*—almost three times their proportion in the population at large" (Brimelow 1995, 7, emphasis his). Brimelow did not note the crimes for which these individuals were incarcerated or what percentage were in federal penitentiaries for immigration violations. Brimelow dedicated an entire section of his book to crime resulting from immigration, drawing first on Ted Robert Gurr, a political scientist at the University of Maryland–College Park, who linked crime waves in 1850, 1900, and 1960 with immigration, though Brimelow was careful to point out that immigration was not the only cause of crime and might not even be a major factor but that it did play a role (Brimelow 1995, 182).

Although Brimelow highlighted the lack of reliable data on crimes committed by immigrants, he cited statistics that were clearly meant to imply a strong linkage between crime and immigrants: 25 percent of the federal prison population were criminal immigrants; 450,000 noncitizens had been convicted of crimes and were in jail or on parole; a May 1990 survey of Los Angeles County jails had found that 18 percent were foreign born and 11 percent had committed deportable offenses; many of those convicted of deportable crimes had never been removed from the United States, and 40 percent had committed further crimes (Brimelow 1995, 183). These statistics sound bad when given without context, but to take one example, although 450,000 noncitizens convicted of crimes sounds like a large number, in 1990 there were, according to the US Census, 19.8 million foreign-born people in the United States, meaning that only about 2 percent of the foreign born were convicted of crimes. Given this context the numbers provided by Brimelow are much less alarming.

But even if immigrants offended at rates no higher than those of the native born, argued Brimelow, "what's the point of immigrants who are no better than we are?" Perhaps acknowledging the weakness of some of the statistics he provided, Brimelow staked part of his contention regarding immigration and crime on what he called "common sense." He pointed out that immigrants were often young men, who were more likely to commit crimes, and in a revival of the 1920s-era linkages between culture and crime he said they were more likely to be from ethnic groups with a "present-orientation" that led to impulsiveness, which in turn made crime more likely among these groups (Brimelow 1995, 184). It is worth quoting Brimelow's own words once again here: "Inevitably, therefore, certain ethnic cultures are more crime prone than others. The numbers can be staggering. For example: Blacks make up only 12 percent of the American population but 64 percent of all violent crime rates" (Brimelow 1995, 184). This link between specific ethnic or racial groups and crime had been refuted in 1931 by the Wickersham Commission, who had specifically examined Mexican immigration and found that even in those areas where Mexicans offended at a higher rate than their proportion of the population, this was often because of factors such as poverty or a lack of understanding of US laws, not the "present-orientation" cited by Brimelow. While Brimelow's comments did not specifically address undocumented immigration or even Mexican immigration, the takeaway was that all immigrants presented law-and-order problems for the United States. This was an echo of a school of thought prevalent in the first two decades of the twentieth century that had tended to see criminality as inherent in the foreign born generally and had driven immigration restriction during that period. Brimelow did mention Mexicans as being involved with "mafias" associated with marijuana, auto theft, and alien smuggling, but he also included Colombians, Hong Kong Chinese, South Koreans, the Chaldeans, and Iraqi Christians as groups with organized mafias. He contended that most Americans had heard little about these groups because of the taboo against saying anything negative about immigration (Brimelow 1995, 185). He would go on to discuss criminal organizations run by Russian Jews and Nigerians as further examples of immigrant groups' predilection for criminality.

Brimelow couched his commentary in a way that was meant to take some of the edge off it. He regularly emphasized, as many restrictionists and bigots have done throughout American history, that his opposition was not to the immigrants themselves but instead to a certain incompatibility between the "new" immigrants and American culture. This is most clearly reflected when Brimelow does specifically talk about undocumented immigration. Rather than criminality, he tries to stress the empathy he has for these individuals. He gives an example of this in the form of a man dragging a young boy whom he "may" have seen on an infrared scope when he shadowed Border Patrol agents. He claims his eyes teared up as he thought of the dangers the boy might have faced and imagined that it could be his son facing the threat of bandits who preyed on these individuals and sold them into child-prostitution rings. This image is shattered by a comment Brimelow makes about sewage that reveals the racism underlying this narrative. He states that the river is filled with raw sewage where he saw the father dragging his son across, and not just any sewage but "Mexican sewage," which then flows into US territory (Brimelow 1995, 239). Pointedly describing the sewage as Mexican sewage, as if there were some fundamental difference in feces south of the border, suggests the differences Brimelow believes there to be between Mexicans and Americans. Even their sewage is worse.

Brimelow's book was not alone in its criticism of immigration's impact on the United States. The controversial book *The Bell Curve,* by the psychologist Richard Herrnstein and the political scientist Charles Murray, discusses the heritable nature of intelligence and the differences in IQ between racial groups. Blacks were found to be a full standard deviation below whites in intelligence, and this, combined with Herrnstein and Murray's theory regarding the heritability of IQ, seemed to suggest that blacks were inferior to whites and that they always would be. The authors of *The Bell Curve* also address immigration, supporting restriction of large-scale immigration because of immigrants' lower intelligence (Herrnstein and Murray 1994). The authors do stress that their argument is not meant to imply race-based differences, but their findings were interpreted that way by many.

Brimelow's screed is indicative of the shift that occurred in thinking about immigration in the 1990s, as there was a turning away from the more balanced rhetoric of IRCA toward something closer to the way immigration had been characterized by men like Representative Box of Texas in the 1920s. The success of Brimelow's books suggests how widespread this belief in immigrant threat was at the time, as a topic many Americans rarely engaged with gained national prominence once again. This renewed prominence was partially driven by an uptick in undocumented immigration in the 1990s. As mentioned earlier, after a fall in the number of undocumented immigrants from 3.2 million in 1986 to 1.9 million in 1988, the undocumented population would reach 3.5 million in 1990. After a small dip in 1992 to 3.4 million, the undocumented population would explode to 5.8 million in 1996, with the combination of media and public attention once again landing it on the policy agenda, as well as likely boosting sales of Brimelow's sensationalist book (Wasem 2012).

Nativist reactions were not limited to just academics. During the IIRIRA debate in the House, Representative Anthony Beilenson of California stated, "With twice as many people here in this country, and then more than twice as many, we can expect to have at least twice as much crime, twice as much congestion, twice as much poverty, twice as many problems in educating our children, providing health care and everything else" (142nd Cong. Rec., 2365). This was very similar to the argument being made by Brimelow regarding immigration, though of course in the case of IIRIRA the target of the rhetoric was undocumented immigration, while Brimelow's broadside had been aimed at immigration more generally.

Thus, as 1996 neared, several factors drove the convergence of immigration law and criminal penalties. The critical failure of IRCA delegitimized a more liberal approach to undocumented immigration; at the same time, IRCA's shortcomings guaranteed that the undocumented population would continue to increase. Spikes in immigration rates in the 1990s, falling white birthrates, and an increasing Latino population led to increased nativism. Finally, there was a continued shift that had begun in the 1980s away from rehabilitation and toward punishment for criminal infractions. Bill Clinton drew on fears of victimhood in his first presidential bid and over the course of his presidency, with being "tough on crime" a focus of his campaign (Beinart 2015). The 1994 Violent Crime Control and Law Enforcement Act put more police on the street; built more prisons; increased the number of federal offenses that could result in the death penalty; added new federal offenses; and mandated a three-strike rule for violent felons (Violent Crime Control and Law Enforcement Act of 1994). This would help to drive mass incarceration in the 1990s, a fact which Clinton himself has acknowledged (Alexander 2010; Merica 2015).

Increasing criminal penalties were part of this return to the treatment of undocumented immigration as a law-enforcement issue. A 1994 report by the US Commission on Immigration Reform, also known as the Jordan Commission for its chair, Barbara Jordan, stated that in terms of immigration policy more broadly, "the immediate need is more effective prevention and deterrence of undocumented immigration" (US Commission on Immigration Reform 1994, 3). The Jordan Commission recommended an expansion of the Border Patrol, the increased use of fences, an electronic employment-verification system, greater enforcement of employer penalties for hiring undocumented workers, and a more streamlined deportation process for criminal aliens (US Commission on Immigration Reform 1994). The focus on enforcement was appealing after IRCA, which had expanded funding for the Border Patrol but had focused primarily on the creation of a guest-worker program, amnesty, and employer sanctions. IIRIRA would swing fully in the other direction, emphasizing enforcement above all else, including more consistent enforcement of employer penalties, as recommended by the Jordan Commission.

Attacking undocumented immigration was popular in the 1990s. For example, a *New York Times* article in 1996 noted that "since the Republicans have taken control of the United States House and Senate, . . . it seems as though all Washington has begun grandstanding on the issue" (Raynar 1996). The *New York Times* piece discusses the climate in the United States toward immigrants, both documented and undocumented, in detail, as well as the less sensational realities of immigration in the 1990s. The author cites two very different sides in the immigration debate: "One side looks at crime, failing schools, and soaring welfare spending and sees too many immigrants. The other sees America, the greatest nation on earth, built on the backs of immigrants and still benefiting enormously from the brains, energy and determination (not to speak of low wages) of the next generation of newcomers. Right now, the debate is more emotional than informed. It's all temper tantrums and red-hot sound bites" (Raynar 1996). Undocumented immigrants who entered the United States illegally, in direct and deliberate violation of the law, were unlikely to garner much sympathy from the American public, no matter what their reason was for coming. Criminal aliens were even worse off. Their criminal convictions ensured even less sympathy from the public and little interest in their fate on the part of politicians. Both groups made convenient scapegoats for the government, which could use their punishment as a performance for the American people. Like crime, immigration policy has ready optics associated with enforcement in the form of border fences and expansion of the INS and the Border Patrol. Even if these failed to stop undocumented immigration, they provided something concrete for politicians seeking to appeal to concerns about "illegal aliens" to show to the American public.

IIRIRA helped further the link between immigration and crime in the post-IRCA period in two ways. First the act allowed undocumented immigrants to be held in detention facilities while awaiting their deportation hearings. These long detentions, often in prison facilities, meant that an undocumented immigrant essentially had to serve time while awaiting a hearing on a civil violation. Those in deportation proceedings also had no right to state-appointed counsel, so they had to either represent themselves or pay for a lawyer. Second, under section 287(g) of IIRIRA, the attorney general could enter into agreements with states to allow their agents to perform "the investigatory, arrest and detention functions of an immigration officer" with federal oversight (Miller 2003, 627). The use of local law enforcement to enforce immigration law illustrated not only the increasing overlap of immigration and criminal law but also the increasing marginalization of undocumented immigrants. If local law enforcement was given the ability to enforce immigration law, those who were in the country illegally would be less likely to report crimes perpetrated against themselves or others. Like S. 5094, IIRIRA severely penalized those who were present in the United States without status (either because of undocumented entry or a visa overstay) by making them ineligible to reenter the country. If someone had been "unlawfully present" in the United States for 180 days, they could not legally reenter for three years; if they had been undocumented for a year or more, they could not legally reenter for ten years. In neither case was there a right of appeal. IIRIRA also authorized the hiring of five thousand new Border Patrol agents and an twelve hundred new INS agents to help tackle undocumented immigration, as well as the second and third tiers of a fourteen-mile fence on the US-Mexico border near San Diego ("White House Calls the Shots" 1996).

Like IRCA, IIRIRA originated as an attempt at more comprehensive reform to address both legal and illegal immigration, but it became clear that the legislation had little prospect of passage if it tried to tackle both. A floor amendment in the House struck out most of the changes to legal immigration, while in the Senate the original bill (S. 1664) was split in half. During the final House-Senate conference on the bill, there was also consideration of a House proposal that would have allowed states to deny public schooling to undocumented immigrants. This was similar in intent to California's Proposition 187, which denied an array of social services to undocumented immigrants to supposedly limit the burden these individuals placed on American taxpayers. The inclusion of this provision might very well have doomed IIRIRA, but ultimately it was left out, despite the Republican presidential candidate Bob Dole's desire to retain it in order to claim that Democrats were soft on immigration. IIRIRA would eventually be rolled into an omnibus spending bill (H.R. 3610) after being stripped of its remaining provisions regarding legal immigration ("White House Calls the Shots" 1996).

Framing Immigration: IIRIRA in the House

The number of references to immigrant criminality in the House debate on IIRIRA reflects the shift away from the relatively liberal programs of IRCA toward the more draconian crime-control-oriented policies of IIRIRA. The criminal threat frame was common throughout the House debate, with a particular focus on the links between undocumented immigration and drugs. Speaking on behalf of her constituents in Utah, Representative Enid Waldholtz stated that they were "having a critical problem with illegal aliens dealing in drugs, that are involved in criminal activities, especially drug trafficking." She claimed that in 1996, of the thirty-six hundred people arrested in Salt Lake City for felony-level drug violations 80 percent were undocumented immigrants (142nd Cong. Rec., pg. 2449). Republican Lamar Smith of Texas stated, "We look at the drugs coming across, the flow, and on those drug ride-alongs, 99 percent have involved illegal immigrants" (142nd Cong. Rec., 2380). Smith also said that "illegal aliens are 10 times more likely than Americans as a whole to have been convicted of a federal crime. Think about the cost to the criminal justice system, including incarceration. But most of all, think about the cost in pain and suffering to the innocent victims and their families" (142nd Cong. Rec., 2379). This later statement suggested a tendency on the part of undocumented immigrants not just to criminality but to violent criminality. The phrase "innocent victims and their families" suggests assault, homicide, and other acts of violence, which were not suggested in any of the earlier debates I examined except for one mention of the potential violence of coyotes in debate on Johnson-Reed. Representative Greg Laughlin of Texas also drew on the criminality narrative in pushing for the second and third tiers of the border fence, arguing that it was not "just stopping illegal immigrants. It was safety for the officers, safety for the people. The rapes, the robberies, the drug sales, and the murders went down because of the fence" (142nd Cong. Rec., 2451).

Republican Marge Roukema of New Jersey, following up on the comments made by Lamar Smith, argued that in addition to increased crime rates, a host of costs were associated with illegal immigration, including lost jobs and the burden imposed on the welfare, education, and health care systems (142nd Cong. Rec., 2380). Another Republican, Representative Brian Bilbray of California, mixed the narrative of immigrant crime with a narrative of concern for the immigrants themselves, saying that he had "to live in my community not only with the crime, the destruction that has occurred from uncontrolled immigration and crime activity along the border, but also a human misery that is being imposed on the illegal immigrants. Our freeways are the scene of many people being slaughtered because smugglers are encouraging illegals to enter our country down the middle of freeways" (142nd Cong. Rec., 2391). This blending of the narrative of immigrant criminality with one of concern, or at least sympathy, for immigrants broadly conceived came up more than once in the debate over H.R. 2202.

Later in the debate, another representative, Republican Dana Rohrabacher of California, mixed statements of concern with thinly veiled threat narratives: "Some people may be deprived overseas, but we are not going to let criminals come into our society and commit crimes and not have our government act upon it and see our jails being filled with illegal aliens. Yeah, we love older people from other countries . . . but we do not want senior citizens coming into America and draining all of the resources. . . . Yes, we care about sick people wherever they come from. We do not want sick people coming here from every corner of the world breaking down our health care system" (142nd Cong. Rec., 2393). Rohrabacher thus expressed compassion while also pressing for greater restriction in immigration policy, particularly concerning undocumented immigrants. Another Republican, Representative Randy Tate of Washington, would tie the lax enforcement of immigration law explicitly to future criminal acts: "Our current law sends the wrong message to would-be illegal immigrants—you won't be penalized for breaking United States law. It is no wonder many so-called illegal immigrants are drawn to crime once they reach our country." Tate cited the specific crimes illegal immigrants were associated with, "bank fraud, credit fraud, check kiting, false marriages, assault, extortion, and drug dealing" (142nd Cong. Rec., 2457). Tate's suggestion was that the lack of immigration enforcement conditioned undocumented immigrants to criminal behavior, since they would perceive that US laws would not be enforced.

Republican John Doolittle of California related a personal anecdote regarding the potential criminality of the undocumented and the lack of protection for American citizens: "The first drive-by shooting in a rural town in my district was committed by an illegal alien. He was convicted and served his sentence, and within one week after he was deported, he was back in the country. Now, it turned out he had committed another crime." According to Doolittle, 98 percent of criminal undocumented immigrants returned after deportation and 40 percent of these committed further crimes, though he did not state where exactly his numbers were from (142nd Cong. Rec., 2477). Similarly, Representative Greg Ganske, a Republican from Iowa, cited the stabbing of a local boy at a party in his district in his support for the 287(g) program included in IIRIRA (142nd Cong. Rec., 2477).

As table 2.2 shows, the number of mentions of the criminal threat frame in the House debate for H.R. 2202, 46, was many times greater than the number for any of the other bills examined. This number nearly tied the number of mentions of the economic threat frame, which was 50. Use of the term *illegal* was eliminated from the coding since the term was regularly used by both those supporting and those opposing IIRIRA, suggesting that it had become the common term for undocumented immigration. However, the economic threat frame was mentioned by only 28 representatives, while the criminal threat frame was mentioned by 32, meaning that for all intents and purposes the two frames were tied.

TABLE 2.2. Threat frames in the House IIRIRA debate: Unique mentions / number of representatives mentioning

FRAME	MENTIONS / REPRESENTATIVES
Positive economic	1 / 1
Negative economic	49 / 28
Positive cultural	3 / 3
Negative cultural	2 / 1
Positive criminal	2 / 2
Negative criminal (excluding *illegal*)	46 / 32

Positive frames were nearly absent from the debate on IIRIRA, with 1 mention of the positive economic contributions of undocumented immigrants, 3 mentions of positive cultural attributes, and 1 mention of a tendency to abide by the law. These were fewer positive characterizations than for any of the other pieces of legislation analyzed, apart from S. 5094, which was also highly punitive in nature. The defenses of the character of undocumented immigrants present in the IRCA debate were replaced with a litany of attacks on the undocumented population as criminals and an economic threat. The cultural threat frame was all but absent from the debate over IIRIRA.

IIRIRA in the Senate

The debate on the Senate version of H.R. 2202—S. 1664—was similar in tone to the debate in the House. Characterizations of undocumented immigrations were mostly negative, though the descriptions of crime were not quite as sensational as those in the House. Regarding criminality, the Senate seemed more concerned with document fraud than with drug trafficking or violent crime, with the bulk of comments on crime citing concerns about the use of fraudulent documents to obtain employment, which had increased exponentially after passage of IRCA (Tichenor 2002; Chishti, Meissner, and Bergeron 2011). In the Senate, there were more mentions of the criminality frame than of the economic threat frame, as well as a larger number of senators mentioning the criminality frame (table 2.3).

Table 2.3 shows that in the Senate as in the House, comments regarding undocumented immigrants tended to be overwhelmingly negative, with only one positive cultural framing and no positive economic or criminal framings. As in the House debate, there were almost no mentions of the cultural threat frame, which was referred to only once dur-

TABLE 2.3. Threat frames in the Senate IIRIRA debate: Unique mentions / number of senators mentioning

FRAME	MENTIONS / SENATORS
Positive economic	0/0
Negative economic	20/12
Positive cultural	1/1
Negative cultural	2/2
Positive criminal	0/0
Negative criminal (excluding *illegal*)	23/14

ing the Senate debate. Criminal aliens were mentioned many times in the Senate debate, though only mentions in which they were specifically referred to as illegal immigrants were coded. A comment by Republican senator Spencer Abraham of Michigan is indicative of the concern about criminal aliens in the Senate debate, though these individuals were not necessarily undocumented: "By conservative estimates, almost half a million felons are living in this country illegally. These aliens have been convicted of murder, rape, drug trafficking, potentially such crimes as espionage, sabotage, treason and/or a number of other serious crimes and are therefore, under the current laws of our country, deportable" (142nd Cong. Rec., 3328).

While there were serious concerns about both criminal aliens and undocumented immigrants, Democrats called for some measure of caution in approaching criminality and undocumented status. Senator Russ Feingold of Wisconsin argued that immigration was a common wedge issue used by politicians to divide people "along racial, ethnic and cultural lines," while Senator Ted Kennedy noted that simply increasing penalties for undocumented immigration would have little effect if the root causes were not addressed, particularly the pull factor of employment (142nd Cong. Rec., 4035, 4486). These comments evidently convinced very few, however, as IIRIRA would pass and become law on September 30, 1996.

IRCA and IIRIRA: Different Discourses for Different Decades

A striking difference between the debate on IRCA and that on IIRIRA has to do with how undocumented immigrants were characterized. During debate on IRCA the term *undocumented* was used 55 times in describing immigrants; *illegal* was used more often (176 times during debate), though in some cases the same member would use both terms interchangeably. In the debate on IIRIRA the term *illegal* was used 467 times in describing the undocumented population, compared with a paltry 20 uses of the term *undocumented*. In debate on IRCA, *undocumented* was used in characterizing immigrants 23 percent of the time, while *illegal* was used 77 percent of the time. During the IIRIRA debate, *undocumented* was used only 4 percent of the time, while *illegal* was used 96 percent of the time. Although this difference may seem innocuous, its importance becomes clear when the characterization of the immigrants themselves is considered.

During the congressional debate on IRCA, the contributions of undocumented immigrants were emphasized, and many went out of their way to humanize this population, pointing out the draw of better-paying jobs and the promise of a better life. Much of the ire in the IRCA debate was directed not at immigrants but at employers, as were the penalties aimed at reducing undocumented immigration. There were many mentions of the pull factors that drew undocumented workers to the United States and many calls on members of Congress to consider that these immigrants came not with the intent of being a burden on the state but instead to work, and work hard, in the hopes of improving their lives or the lives of their families. The exploitation these individuals experienced was mentioned multiple times, and one of the stated purposes of IRCA was to end this exploitation, to bring immigrants out of the shadows, so that many of the problems associated with undocumented immigration would be addressed.

The IIRIRA debate was the polar opposite. There was little mention of the culpability of the employer, and even the Jordan Commission's recommendation that new legislation address problems in enforcement of the employer penalties was largely ignored in the legislation itself. Almost any reference to the undocumented population was to "illegals" or "illegal aliens/immigrants." This difference in the terminology used was matched by a marked difference in how undocumented immigrants were portrayed. Gone were the representations of this group as hardworking, family-oriented people who in many ways resembled the immigrants of yore, those groups of Irish, Italians, Poles, Jews, and Germans who had come to the United States to work hard and make a better life for themselves. Instead, most mentions of undocumented immigrants not only referred to them as lawbreakers but went further, describing them as drug dealers and criminals. Lurid accounts of murder and shootings were used to show the necessity for draconian controls.

All of this despite ample evidence suggesting no linkage between criminality and legal status (Lee, Martinez, and Rosenfeld 2001; Padgett

2010; Wadsworth 2010). In fact, many studies have found a relationship between immigration and criminality that is opposite the one usually suggested. In 2001, Lee, Martinez, and Rosenfeld looked at homicide rates in three border cities with large immigrant communities and high levels of immigration between 1985 and 1995. Examining 352 neighborhood census tracts in Miami, El Paso, and San Diego, the authors found that the percentage of new immigrants in these tracts had no relationship to homicide rates, except for El Paso. In the case of El Paso, the effect was negative rather than positive, so the higher the percentage of new immigrants in the neighborhood, the lower the likelihood of homicide. The only consistent predictor of homicide in all three cities was, unsurprisingly, poverty. In a study of homicides in San Diego from 1980 to 2000, Martinez, Stowell, and Lee (2010) found that as in El Paso, neighborhood homicide rates in San Diego were negatively associated with the percentage of foreign born in the community. Both studies provide strong evidence that immigration and homicide rates, if they are related at all, tend to be linked in a relationship opposite the one frequently touted by those looking to justify draconian immigration policies. That is, immigration into neighborhoods, at least in border cities, tends to lead to a decrease in homicides.

Both studies mentioned above are specific to border cities, so perhaps immigration is related to crime in cities other than these. After all, as I argued in chapter 1, the relationship the Dillingham Commission report on crime and the foreign born found between changes in the character of crime and immigration was not generalizable because the data it relied on were drawn from only a handful of geographic regions. The same can be said of the two studies cited above. Tim Wadsworth (2010) addressed this shortcoming by examining homicide and robbery rates in 459 cities across the United States with populations of fifty thousand or more. Wadsworth analyzed the effect of the percentage of foreign born in a city, as well as the effect of the proportion of these individuals who were new immigrants to the United States, having arrived in the last five years, through both an ordinary-least-squares regression (OLS) and a pooled cross-sectional time-series model. The former allows the influence of immigration on crime to be examined for 1990 and 2000 independently, while the pooled time-series model allows the effect of changes in immigration on crime to be assessed. For the OLS regression, Wadsworth found that in 1990 there was a positive relationship between the percentage of foreign born in each city and its homicide rates, though there was no relationship between new immigration and homicide. These findings were the same for robbery in 1990, with the percentage of foreign born correlated with a larger number of robberies, while the proportion of new immigrants had no effect. However, in 2000 the OLS model found no relationship between the percentage of foreign born or the proportion of new immigrants and homicide. The only positive relationship found was between the size of the foreign-born population and robbery.

Turning to the pooled time-series model, Wadsworth (2010) found no evidence that changes in the percentage of foreign born between 1990 and 2000 influenced homicide. There was an inverse relationship between the percentage of new immigrants in a city and homicide rates, a finding that echoes those of Lee et al. (2001) in El Paso and Martinez et al. (2010) in San Diego. The larger the increase in the percentage of new immigrants between 1990 and 2000, the lower the likelihood of homicide. For robbery, a similarly inverse relationship was found, with the change in the new immigrant population having no effect on robbery rates but change in the size of the foreign-born population leading to decreases in robbery rates on average.

The data suggest that there is no relationship between immigration and crime, whether specific cities or a broader sample is examined. There is in fact no evidence, other than anecdotal evidence, of any relationship between immigration and crime. Research has shown that even in the much-maligned sanctuary cities, where federal immigration detainers may be ignored and therefore undocumented immigrants do not have to fear deportation should they commit certain crimes, there is no relationship between sanctuary status and crime rates (Gonzalez O'Brien, Collingwood, and El-Khatib 2017; Lyons, Velez, and Santoro 2013). A number of studies have found that crime rates among native-born Americans are higher than those for the foreign born in the United States (see, e.g., Martinez and Lee 2000). This makes sense when one considers that an American citizen does not need to fear deportation in addition to criminal charges for any illegal behavior, while undocumented immigrants do.

Many of the studies cited above were conducted long after passage of IIRIRA, but studies dating from as early as 1931 looked at the relationship between crime and immigration. In 1994, just two years before IIRIRA passed, the US Commission on Immigration Reform issued an interim report stating that crime rates in border cities with high levels of immigration, such as El Paso, were lower than in nonborder cities (US Commission on Immigration Reform 1994). Yet despite this spurious relationship between immigration and crime, IIRIRA marked an about-face in how undocumented immigration was discussed and a return to the path of the 1929–85 period, in which undocumented immigration was viewed through the lens of criminality. Crime-control tactics— deterrence through punishment and increases in the size of the Border Patrol—were seen as the solution. Through its promise of enforcement, IIRIRA became a valuable political symbol, or as Newton puts it, "The utility of IIRAIRA lay in the theater of government activity" (Newton 2008, 135). But a simple increase in enforcement failed to address the myriad factors that contributed to undocumented immigration, although it was safe policy. Like the shift from rehabilitation to punishment in incarceration during the severity revolution, IIRIRA was motivated by a recognition that symbolic politics often resonates more with the American public than does policy aimed at resolving the problem in the long term (Simon 2001, 2007). Politicians who backed IIRIRA could point to the increasing number of undocumented immigrants sitting in detention facilities as an example of policy success even if this had little real significance for resolving the problem undocumented immigration in the long term. Detentions and deportations can be easily cited as examples of progress and being "tough on crime."

As mentioned earlier, because of the convergence of a number of factors, IRCA came at a moment of punctuated equilibrium in the history of immigration policy, when a rejection of the politics of scapegoating was a real possibility. When the programs it established came up short, IRCA became a critical policy failure and there was a return to the policies of old. Once again, the responsibility for the "problem" of undocumented immigration was shifted almost entirely onto the immigrants themselves, who were portrayed as potentially dangerous criminals. Path dependence can function not only at the level of the policies passed or the relative ease or difficulty with which this occurs but also at the level of policy discourse. Undocumented immigration had long been discussed as a crime-control issue and immigrants had long been scapegoated as potential criminals. IRCA represented a change in both policy and discourse, but both returned to criminalization when IRCA failed to stop undocumented immigration. In fact, the rhetoric of criminality under IIRIRA became even more pronounced than it had been in any of the legislation discussed above.

IIRIRA brought no return to policies acknowledging both the value of undocumented labor and the responsibility of both the immigrant and the employer. Instead there has been increasing criminalization in the post-9/11 environment, with the formation of ICE, which has posted record-breaking numbers of deportations year after year, even during the first few years of the Obama administration, with 419,384 deportations for fiscal year 2012, though this dropped to 368,644 in 2013, after Obama directed ICE to focus on criminal immigrants (Epstein 2014; Gonzalez 2013; Pew Research Center 2014). Debates on Arizona's Senate bill 1070 in 2010, which would have allowed local police to ask for proof of citizenship during routine stops, and clone laws passed in a number of states afterwards illustrate the enduring legacy of IIRIRA and the reinvigoration of the nativist discourse of immigrant criminality, as well as the historical significance of the shortcomings of IRCA. Polls showed high levels of support for Senate bill 1070 despite the likelihood of racial profiling, and the rhetoric used by Jan Brewer and other supporters of the law and its clones echoed many of the statements made by supporters of IIRIRA in 1996 (Pew Research Center 2012). Undocumented immigrants were linked to the drug war, and often baseless comments were made about the threat they posed to the American people (Milbank 2010). Even political ads capitalized on the perceptions of immigrant criminality, with ads by Republican Senate candidate Sharron Angle of Nevada in 2010 featuring young Latino men skulking around a fence, walking threateningly toward the camera, and featured in fake mug shots in what could be described as gang attire, while noting incumbent Democrat Harry Reid's opposition to Senate bill 1070 (Friends of Sharron Angle 2010). President Trump regularly claimed that sanctuary cities "breed crime" and even once went so far as to declare that most Mexican immigrants were criminals and rapists (Farley 2017; Kopan 2016).

Yet while these representations of undocumented immigrants have become part and parcel of elite discourse on immigration, it remains unclear whether the American public believes these narratives of criminal threat. The media's ability to influence public opinion and the fact that often the most sensational of claims about undocumented immigration are given airtime by the media make it seem likely that at least some part of the public would accept these claims (Kim et al. 2011; Masuoka and Junn 2013; Uwimana 2011). While it can be difficult to determine whether elite rhetoric on immigration drives public opinion, or vice versa, the public certainly takes cues from elites and the media, particularly in those areas where they have little experience (Zaller 1992). Most Americans have an opinion on undocumented immigration regardless of whether there are any undocumented immigrants where they live. These opinions are based on the "pictures in our heads," as well as the stereotypes that attend those images and identifiers (Edelman 1964; Lippmann 1922; Zaller 1992). We are not born knowing what an undocumented immigrant is, any more than we are born with notions of racial catego-ries. These are learned, as are our reactions to them, and in many areas of policy they are in fact based on elite cues. The elites can be journalists, politicians, academics, and government officials who provide the infor-mation on which we based our opinions of issues like undocumented immigration (Zaller 1992). If elites tend to construct undocumented im-migration as a problem of criminality, the public will respond to this, though of course divisions in elite rhetoric will also lead to divisions in public opinion.

With the exception of IRCA, almost from the beginning undocu-mented immigration has been constructed as an issue of criminality. Depending on the point in time, uncertainty about the identity of im-migrants entering the United States illegally led to fears that they might be communists, anarchists, drug dealers, gang members, or terrorists. Undocumented entry was taken by some to imply a greater disposition toward criminality. In 2017, the president of the United States continues to regularly characterize the undocumented as dangerous criminals and advocates the building of a physical barrier between the United States and Mexico to keep them out. This has undoubtedly colored both the ste-reotypes many Americans have of undocumented immigrants and their policy preferences. The frames discussed above help determine " what the public thinks it is becoming informed about, which often determines how people takes sides on political issues" (Zaller 1992). With undocu-mented immigration framed as a crime-control issue by elites and media, it is very likely that a large percentage of the American public believe that this is exactly what undocumented immigration is. While the con-vergence between criminal law and immigration policy has been docu-mented in the preceding pages, two questions remain to be addressed: Do the American people believe the narratives of immigrant criminality so frequently used by Congress to justify draconian immigration poli-cies, and do their beliefs have an effect on their policy preferences?

THREE

Immigrant Criminality and Public Opinion

As the preceding chapters show, congressional debates have long relied on narratives of immigrant criminality to construct undocumented immigration as a crime-control issue. The congressional framing of undocumented immigration has also had a significant impact on how the media cover it, not because of elite rhetoric during congressional debates, to which the media are unlikely to pay much attention, but instead because of the legislation that has resulted. Senate bill 5094, INS initiatives like Mexican Repatriation and Operation Wetback, and IIRIRA all have influenced what the media and the American public are exposed to regarding undocumented immigration. Arrests, raids, and pursuits of undocumented immigrants by the Border Patrol suggest criminality and are the main focus of media stories on immigration (Drier and Tabak 2009; Kim et al. 2011; Masuoka and Junn 2013; Uwimana 2011). This criminal threat frame, even if not verbally mentioned in stories, is visually referenced—a direct result of legislation that has increasingly criminalized undocumented immigration. We can think of congressional legislation as part of a feedback loop in which the rhetoric of crime control influences legislation passed by Congress, which in turn influences enforcement actions taken by agencies like the INS/ICE. These enforcement actions then help to shape media coverage and framing of the issue, which influences public opinion on immigration, which in turn reinforces congressional treatment of undocumented immigration as a crime-control issue.

Media also provide elites an easy means to communicate their positions to the public and play an important role in the formation of public opinion on issues like undocumented immigration through agenda setting and framing. The amount of coverage issues receive in the media help to determine which issues people think are important (Iyengar and Simon 1993; Scheufele 2000; Scheufele and Tewksbury 2007). It is arguable that outside of those individuals in border states or areas with large immigrant communities, most members of the public have little reason to think about immigration. If they do think about it, it is probably because they have been told that it is an issue, through either media coverage or elite messaging. Framing also plays an important role in opinion formation. If the media regularly frame undocumented immigration as a law-and-order issue, this will be how members of the public tend to view it. Media framing in turn can be dependent on how a policy issue has been constructed by elites, from whom the media sometimes take cues in framing a story (Schnell 2001; Zaller and Chiu 1996). If Congress has, through bills like IIRIRA, made undocumented immigration a crime-control issue, that is how the media will tend to discuss it.

An example of this tendency is the controversy that erupted around sanctuary cities in 2015. Then candidate Donald Trump heavily criticized San Francisco's sanctuary policy as being responsible for the death of Kathryn Steinle, who was shot by an undocumented immigrant who had been released by San Francisco because of its policy to ignore ICE detainer requests for low-level offenders. Most Americans were likely unaware that San Francisco was a sanctuary city prior to Steinle's death and Trump's criticism. Indeed, most Americans were likely unaware of what a sanctuary city was, since despite their politically controversial nature, they are rarely discussed in mainstream media unless an event focuses attention on them. On the heels of the shooting and the comments made by Donald Trump, a Rasmussen Reports poll found that 62 percent of Americans wanted the Justice Department to take legal action against sanctuary cities (Rasmussen Reports 2015).

These opinions on sanctuary policy were formed on the basis of framing of San Francisco's sanctuary status as being directly responsible for Steinle's death. Much of the media coverage of sanctuary cities in the days following the shooting on July 1, was, unsurprisingly, about this tragedy. For many Americans, this was the first they had heard about sanctuary cities, and so they linked them to crime. The response to the Steinle shooting was an example of the role played by media in spreading elite messaging that linked criminality and the threat of violence to undocumented immigration. Declarations of the criminal threat posed by undocumented immigrants had also been used in 2010 by Jan Brewer to justify Arizona's Senate bill 1070, which would have allowed police to request proof of citizenship from those they suspected might be undocumented immigrants had most of the law not been struck down by the Supreme Court, earning it the nickname "driving while Latino" law. Brewer claimed that most undocumented immigrants were drug mules and associated with cartels (Sanchez 2010). The support for Senate bill 1070 was surprisingly strong in the period following its passage despite opponents' warning of the danger of racial profiling that would result from the law. Brewer's claims of dangers from drugs and cartel violence, including one claim that headless bodies were being found in the desert, no doubt helped garner support for the bill (Milbank 2010). One clone version of Senate bill 1070 would have taken the explicit racism of the bill one step further by not allowing Canadians and Europeans to simply present a passport to prove their legality, an option not available to Mexicans (Elfrink 2010).

Research on media coverage of undocumented immigration has found it to be largely negative and to emphasize enforcement operations, which means that this is what the public is most frequently exposed to (Abrajano and Singh 2009; Akdenizli et al. 2008; Chavez 2008; Kim et al. 2011; Masuoka and Junn 2013 Santa Ana 2002). Stories about undocumented immigration often feature images of arrests and ICE raids, which visually suggest criminality regardless of the content of the story. Stories on undocumented immigration also often use language suggestive of threat, comparing it to an "invasion" or "flood" (Chavez 2008; Santa Ana 2002). This negative visual framing is likely to have an impact on public perceptions of immigrant criminality.

Of course, elite discourse also plays a role in public opinion, so when high-profile figures like Arizona governor Jan Brewer or Donald Trump emphasize the criminality of the undocumented, this can forge or reinforce a mental linkage between crime and undocumented immigration. This pairing of concepts or issues with a group or individual, leading to an association between the two, is a form of priming (Iyengar and Kinder 1987; Scheufele and Tewksbury 2007). Many members of the public have been primed by media and elite discourse to think of crime when undocumented immigration is mentioned. The overrepresentation of blacks as criminals in the news has influenced how they are perceived, and the same is probably true for undocumented immigrants (Dixon and Azocar 2007). There is some evidence that media portrayals directly influence attitudes toward immigrants, with Schemer et al. (2012) finding that people with little or moderate knowledge about immigration were influenced by negative news coverage.

It is important to understand public beliefs about immigration because research has shown strong connections between perceived threat and anti-immigrant attitudes (Fetzer 2000; Stephan et al. 2005; Wilson 2001). A belief that immigrant groups pose an economic or cultural threat has been found to be a strong predictor of favorability toward restrictive immigration policies, something I examine in chapter 4.

Past studies have tended to focus solely on economic and/or cultural threat frames in their examination of anti-immigrant attitudes. With regard to economics, survey questions have asked whether the foreign born take the jobs of the native born, fail to pay taxes, or impose a burden on social services such as education and health care. With regard to culture, they have asked whether immigrants pose a threat to American culture or refuse to learn English (Fetzer 2000; Stephan et al. 2005; Wilson 2001). Perceptions of immigrant criminality have been largely absent from public-opinion surveys, which makes it impossible to assess whether people differ in terms of what affects their agreement or disagreement with the various frames. A 2006 Faces of Immigration study did ask a battery of questions related to "Latino immigration" that covered all three threat frames. Forty-one percent of whites agreed that Latino immigrants often end up on welfare; 38 percent agreed that they increase crime; 38 percent agreed that they keep to themselves and don't try to fit in; and 21 percent agreed that their values conflict with American culture (Masuoka and Junn 2013).

There is evidence that blacks and whites differ in the extent of their anti-immigrant attitudes. Masuoka and Junn (2013), drawing on the Faces of Immigration survey, found that blacks were less likely than whites to subscribe to any of threat frames, apart from the belief that Latino immigrants' values conflict with American culture. On this question, there was only a 1 percent difference between blacks and whites, whereas on all others the difference was in the double digits. While there are more studies on white opinion toward undocumented immigration, recent work on black attitudes finds that overall, negative attitudes are lower among blacks (Brader, Valentino, and Suhay 2008; Masuoka and Junn 2013; Nteta 2013, 2014). Nteta (2014) draws on the same national poll that I used in this study and finds an 11 percent difference between blacks and whites on negative attitudes toward undocumented immigrants; participants were asked to rate their warmth for this group on a feeling thermometer. This difference is likely related to how blacks themselves have tended to be covered in television news, with studies finding that they are overrepresented in stories about crime (Entman 1990, 1994). Research has found that while television news stories about crime increase support for more punitive approaches to crime control and increase negative attitudes toward blacks, this was not found to be the case among black viewers (Gilliam and Iyengar 2000), which suggests that media coverage, specifically when it relates to crime, may be viewed more critically by blacks and therefore play a smaller role in their attitude formation.

Immigrant Threat and Television News

I draw on two surveys conducted in 2011 to examine how the media influence perceptions of immigrant criminality. One, the Multi-state Survey of Race and Politics (MSSRP), conducted from January 24 through March 12, 2011, featured a nationally representative sample of 1,504 adults from 13 states who agreed to participate in a telephone interview. The states were Arizona, California, Colorado, Florida, Georgia, Michigan, Missouri, North Carolina, Nevada, Ohio, Pennsylvania, South Carolina, and Wisconsin. In the survey, 903 individuals self-identified as white, and 379 as black.

A second, smaller survey by the University of Washington Institute for the Study of Ethnicity, Race and Sexuality (WISER) was conducted in the summer of 2011 with a national sample of 802 individuals. Of these 802 individuals, 643 completed the entire survey; 383 of these self-identified as white, and 155 as black. There was some bias in that the sample overrepresented the well educated and wealthy. Summary statistics for the demographic variables in the WISER poll are presented in table A1 in the appendix, while weights were used in the MSSRP poll to account for biases in the data.

Both surveys featured questions on the economic, cultural, and criminal threat frames discussed in the preceding chapters. Participants were asked a battery of immigration questions related to these threat frames and to their policy preferences on undocumented immigration, as well as standard demographic questions. WISER poll participants were also asked whether they recalled hearing the threat statement, or something similar, in the past. Those who said yes were then asked the source of the statement—friend, family member, politician, television, or other media—and their level of agreement. This information helps researchers understand the sources of negative framings of undocumented immigration. Following the threat-frame questions, participants were asked several questions regarding their policy preferences concerning undocumented immigration.

The three threat questions in the 2011 MSSRP poll asked whether those surveyed agreed with collective-threat statements regarding undocumented immigrants, with answers ranging from "strongly disagree" to "strongly agree" on a five-point Likert scale, with a neutral category denoting neither agreement nor disagreement. While the questions in the MSSRP poll were generally about new immigrants, the immigration debate in the United States is largely about undocumented immigration, and it is assumed that this is the group most respondents had in mind when they answered the questions. Valentino, Brader, and Jardina (2013) found that when the ethnicity of an immigrant group was not specified, study participants tended to think of Latinos, which suggests that something similar is happening with the "new" immigrants in the MSSRP poll. Responses were then recoded as dummy variables, with a 1 indicating agreement. Participants were asked if they agreed with the following statements:

New immigrants are a burden because they take up housing, health care, and jobs.

Immigrants today are less willing to adopt the American way of life.

New immigrants have increased crime in the United States.

The 2011 WISER poll featured five collective-threat questions on undocumented immigration—one on the economic threat frame, one on the cultural threat frame, and three on the criminal threat frame. Participants were asked if they agreed with the following:

Illegal immigrants are a burden on the United States because they take housing, health care, or jobs away from others.

The culture of the United States is changing for the worse because of illegal immigration.

Crossing the border is a crime, and immigrants who come to the United States in this way are criminals.

Illegal immigrants are involved with drugs and gangs.

Neighborhoods with lots of illegal immigrants have higher crime rates.

Responses were recoded in a similar fashion to those of the MSSRP poll, with a 1 indicating agreement.

The main independent variable of interest is the impact of media consumption on agreement with the criminal-threat prompts. The MSSRP asked participants if they watched television news programs, and if so, how often. Responses ranged from 1 ("never") to 4 ("often"), but only

14 percent of participants reported watching television news either never or seldom. Because of this, frequency of television news consumption was constructed as a dummy variable, with a 1 indicating that the individual watched television news "often," while all other responses were coded as 0. Sixty-one percent of the sample were coded as frequent television news viewers and 39 percent as less than frequent.

While the influence of the news media was the primary variable of interest, other potential explanations for agreement with the criminal threat frame had to be examined. To assess the impact of underlying psychological predispositions on perceptions of criminal threat, a measure of social-dominance orientation was included in the models. Participants were asked to rate their agreement with each of the following statements:

If certain groups of people stayed in their place, we would have fewer problems.
Inferior groups should stay in their place.
Sometimes other groups must be kept in their place.
We should do what we can to equalize conditions for different groups.
Group equality should be our ideal.
We should increase social equality.

The social-dominance-orientation scale ranges from 1 (low) to 7 (high). Social-dominance orientation is a personality trait that centers on a belief in a hierarchical and zero-sum conceptualization of society, which results in preferences for maintaining existing hierarchies and in-group dominance of out-groups (Pratto et al. 1994; Sidanius 1993; Sidanius and Pratto 2001). This has been shown to be a predictor of both racism and anti-immigrant attitudes and is included to assess the effect of psychological traits on belief in the criminal threat frames (Esses et al. 2001; Pratto et al. 1994; Sidanius 1993; Sidanius and Pratto 2001).

A second possible explanation for perceptions of criminal threat is racism toward Latinos more broadly. Since the debate around undocumented immigration is for the most part about immigrants from Mexico and Central America, a variable was included that measured the relative coolness or warmth of blacks and whites toward Latinos as a group via a feeling thermometer ranging from 1 (unfavorable) to 10 (favorable). This measure was then scaled from -10 to 10, with the scores participants assigned their own racial group subtracted from the score they gave Latinos. The score thus reflected the respondent's warmth toward Latinos in the context of the warmth they felt toward their own group. This resulted in a scale ranging from a -10, denoting a very unfavorable feeling toward Latinos, to 10, denoting a very favorable feeling.

Previous research has shown that knowledge can moderate the effects of racially biased news stories on stereotypes and that individuals with little knowledge were more likely to be affected by racially biased reporting and priming effects (Huber and Lapinski 2006). Based on these findings, a dummy variable was created to measure political knowledge. If respondents answered three questions on American government correctly, they were considered high in political knowledge and coded as 1; all other individuals were coded as 0. The models also included a question on economic anxiety, as well as standard demographic questions on income, education, gender, and political identification.

White Public Opinion and the Undocumented Threat

What first needs to be examined is the rate of agreement with the various criminal threat frames. As mentioned earlier, perceptions of criminality have rarely been examined in previous public-opinion polls, so there is currently little knowledge of public opinion about immigrant criminality. Figure 3.1 shows both whites' and blacks' level of agreement with the criminal threat frames appearing on the MSSRP and WISER polls.

Overall, agreement with all the criminal threat frames ranged from 32 percent (immigrants increase crime in the United States) to 74 percent (crossing the border is a crime). The finding for crime rates matches up with the 2006 Faces of Immigration study, which found that 38 percent of whites agreed that Latino immigrants "significantly increase crime" (Masuoka and Junn 2013). Among self-identified whites, a whopping 74 percent agreed that undocumented entry was a crime and that those who entered in this fashion were therefore criminals. This was the highest level of agreement for any of the threat frames included in the MSSRP or WISER polls. The lowest overall agreement was with the statement that new immigrants increased crime rates in the United States, which was at 32 percent among white respondents. Approximately 46 percent of whites believed that "illegal" immigrants were more likely to be involved with drugs and gangs, and 52 percent agreed that they drove up neighborhood crime rates.

Table 3.1 shows the racial differences in agreement with all threat frames included in the MSSRP and WISER polls. Whites' agreement with the economic threat frame was 38 percent in the MSSRP poll and 66 percent in the WISER poll, ranking second in terms of agreement in

FIGURE 3.1. Percent agreement with threat frames by race

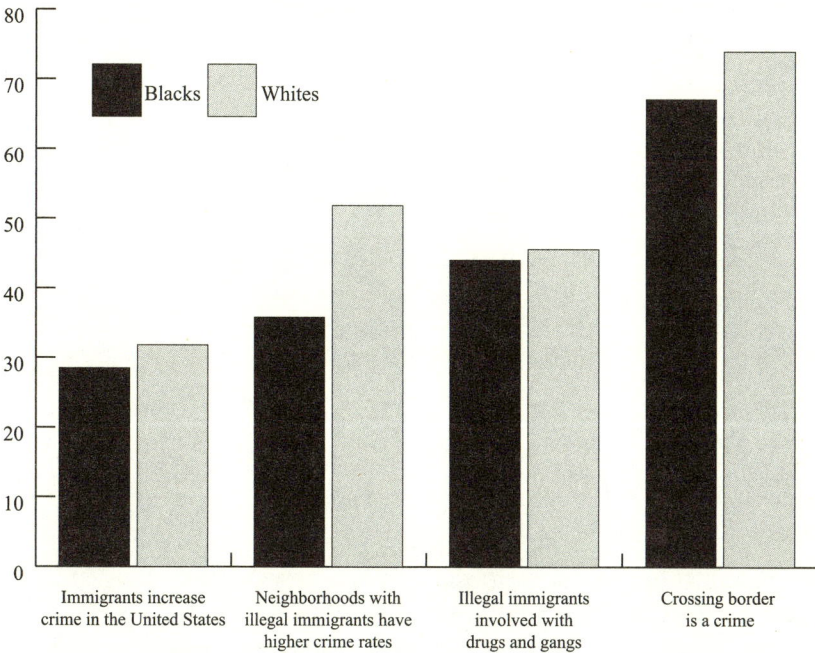

both polls. The cultural threat questions were worded very differently for the two polls. The MSSRP asked whether new immigrants were less likely to adopt the American way of life, which suggests an unwillingness to assimilate, with which 46 percent of whites agreed. The WISER poll asked whether the culture of the United States was worse off because of illegal immigration, and agreement with this harsher statement was lower, at approximately 37 percent.

Black Public Opinion and the Undocumented Threat

Both polls also included an oversample of blacks, presenting a unique opportunity to examine differences between blacks and whites on questions of immigrant criminality. Because of high rates of poverty among blacks, they are more likely to live near Latino immigrant communities and may even compete with individuals from that community for jobs (Alozie and Ramirez 1999; Betancur and Gills 2000; Bobo 1988; Kerr, Miller, and Reid 2000). Approximately 52 percent of blacks voted for California's Proposition 187, which relied heavily on the narrative of criminality to justify cutting undocumented immigrants off from vital social services (R. D. Jacobson 2008). While whites voted for Proposi-

TABLE 3.1. Percentage agreeing with threat questions on the MSSRP and WISER polls, by race

THREAT	WHITES	BLACKS
MSSRP		
Burden on housing, health care, jobs	38	44
Less likely to assimilate	46	35
Increase crime in United States	32	28
WISER		
Burden on housing, health care, jobs	66	49
Change culture for worse	37	27
Crossing is a crime	74	67
Involved with drugs and gangs	46	44
Increase neighborhood crime	52	36

tion 187 in far higher numbers, the split in the black community suggests that there may be a large number of blacks who also subscribe to the criminal threat frame regarding undocumented immigration.

At the same time, blacks have long been victims of the injustices resulting from the criminal threat frame. Negative depictions of blacks in the news, in the movies, and on television shows have helped to craft an image of young black men as inherently dangerous (Alexander 2010; Entman 1990, 1994; Mendelberg 2001; Russell-Brown 1998; Welch 2007). Because blacks themselves have been portrayed in a manner suggesting increased criminality, they may recognize the criminal threat frame for what it is and therefore agree with it less often than their white peers.

Table 3.1 shows that this is only the case for some of the criminal threat frames. When asked whether undocumented immigrants were likely to be involved with drugs and gangs, blacks and whites differed by only 1.6 percent. Similarly, for the question on the MSSRP poll asking whether immigrants increased crime in the United States, there was only a marginal, 3 percent difference between black and white agreement, suggesting that blacks and whites differ little in the criminal stereotypes they hold of the undocumented population. On the other two questions on the WISER poll, opinion diverged significantly. When asked whether crossing the border without documents was a crime and whether those who did so were criminals, blacks agreed at a lower rate than whites, 67 percent compared with 74 percent, a seven-point difference. On the question whether undocumented immigrants increase neighborhood crime rates, the difference was even larger, with 52 percent of whites and only 36 percent of blacks agreeing.

One potential reason for this difference between blacks and whites on the question of neighborhood crime rates could be that this framing personalizes the question, priming the respondent to think about undocumented immigrants or Latinos in their local context. Since blacks are more likely than whites to live in multiracial neighborhoods with Latino residents, they may have a more realistic picture of the effect of undocumented immigrants on crime rates (Gay 2006; Glaeser and Vigdor 2001; Logan 2001). In addition, white fears of crime have been shown to be linked not to the crime rate in their area but to the size of the nonwhite population. As the size of this population increases, white fears of victimhood also increase, regardless of the trend in the crime rate for things like burglary or robbery (Quillian and Pager 2010). Quillian and Pager (2010) found that a similar linkage was not found for nonwhites, suggesting that in the case of the question about neighborhood crime rates, whites might be responding on the basis of a perceived racial threat because of the growth of the Latino population in their neighborhood or simply because they have little or no experience of living in a multiracial neighborhood. The latter reason would similarly make racial threat the likely explanation for the divergence in black and white public opinion, since whites with little or no experience of living near undocumented immigrants or Latinos might be responding to the question based on what they think would happen in their neighborhood if undocumented immigrants lived there.

The similarity between blacks and whites on the question of immigrant criminality is surprising. Similar percentages of blacks and whites agreed that the undocumented were likely to be involved with drugs or gangs or to drive up crime in the United States. Even on the question whether undocumented crossing of the border was a crime and the undocumented, criminals, a majority of blacks agreed, though their percentage was lower than the percentage of whites who agreed. Clearly, the criminalization of undocumented immigration has been effective. Most blacks and whites in the United States today agree that undocumented crossing is a crime and that anyone who does so is a criminal, which according to S. 5094 is factually accurate. The WISER poll demonstrates that not only are most Americans aware of this fact but they agree with it, which will complicate any attempts at comprehensive immigration reform. Indeed, those who agreed with this frame were much more likely to support deportation and felony charges for undocumented immigrants and less likely to support a path to citizenship.

On the other threat frames included in the two polls, fewer blacks than whites tended to agree that undocumented immigrants changed US culture for the worse (27% compared with 37%) and that they did not assimilate as past immigrant groups had (35% compared with 46%). The findings in regard to the economic threat frames included in the MSSRP and WISER polls were mixed despite the similarity of the questions. In the MSSRP poll, more blacks (44%) than whites (38%) agreed that new immigrants were an economic burden on the United States, but on the WISER poll far more whites (66%) than blacks (49%) agreed. One potential explanation for this difference was the size of the oversamples. Only 155 blacks were included in the WISER poll, compared with 344 in the larger MSSRP poll.

Considering that some low-income blacks might compete with Latino immigrants for jobs and share the same neighborhood, this finding make a fair amount of sense (Gay 2006; Glaeser and Vigdor 2001; Logan 2001). Overall, blacks were slightly less likely than whites to agree with the criminal threat frames, though in some cases the difference was marginal, or with the cultural threat frames but more likely to see immigrants as an economic or political threat.

The Role of Media in Perceptions of Criminality

There is ample evidence that a substantial number of Americans, regardless of race, subscribe to the immigrant-as-criminal narrative. The lowest level of agreement for the criminal threat frames in the MSSRP and WISER polls was approximately 30 percent, meaning that even for the least popular of the frames, approximately one-third of all respondents agreed. This is worrying for a country that needs comprehensive immigration reform, which ultimately will have to include some path to legal residence or citizenship for the roughly eleven million undocumented immigrants already in the country. A perception that these individuals are criminals, increase crime, or are involved with drugs or gangs will make any debate over a path to citizenship politically fraught, particularly if the path includes any kind of amnesty program for those already in the country, as IRCA did in 1986.

It is therefore important to understand why people believe that undocumented immigrants are criminals or drive up crime rates. As shown in the preceding chapters, in congressional rhetoric and policy making, undocumented immigration has been constructed as a crime-control issue since 1929. Thus, most immigration-enforcement actions by ICE resemble law-enforcement operations, which has influenced how media cover the issue. Media coverage tends to show undocumented immigrants being handcuffed and taken into ICE custody or footage of the raids themselves (Drier and Trabak 2009). In a 2011 study, Fujioka found that negative news images of Latino immigrants led to more anti-immigrant attitudes among black and white college students, showing how effective media coverage can be in influencing attitudes. This coverage often caricatures the undocumented visually, regardless of its actual tone, because all the viewer is exposed to is images that prime thoughts of crime and criminality. News media are also responsible for the dissemination of political rhetoric on undocumented immigration, and the more sensational statements, such as Donald Trump's comments about Mexican immigrants being rapists and criminals, tend to get the most coverage. Because of the relatively one-sided portrayal of undocumented immigration in cable and local news, it is expected that those who report being frequent television news viewers will be more likely to associate undocumented immigrants with criminality.

One way of determining the role of media, a way that has not been employed in previous studies on immigration attitudes, is to ask respondents if they recall hearing a given threat statement before, and if so, from where. The 2011 WISER poll asked participants if they had heard a given statement from friends, family, television, a politician, another media source, or elsewhere. These sources were collapsed into four categories: media, politicians, friends or family, and elsewhere. A majority of respondents reported that they heard economic, cultural, and criminal threat statements about immigration from either television or some other media source, suggesting that the most common source for negative frames in regard to undocumented immigration was the media.

Across all three criminal threat frames, more than 50 percent of both blacks and whites reported hearing a given statement from some media source. There was little difference between blacks and whites regarding where they had heard the various threat frames, though a slightly larger percentage of blacks gave the media as their source. The second most frequently reported source was "somewhere else," while friends and family came in a distant third. These findings make sense considering that news media are the main source of information on issues like immigration and the main avenue for political elites to communicate their message to the public (Zaller 1992). Undocumented immigration may be more of a topic of discussion between friends and family in states where this issue is highly salient, such as border states, but research has shown that in immigration-salient states there is also more media coverage and that it tends to be more negative (Branton and Dunaway 2009). Because of the imagery and negative rhetoric often associated with coverage of undocumented immigration, members of the public are being exposed to largely negative tropes regarding immigrant criminality through the media. This statement is supported by past studies on the tenor of coverage typically afforded undocumented immigrants, which have found it to be negative for the most part (Abrajano and Singh 2009; Branton et al. 2011; Chavez 2008; Kim et al. 2011; Masuoka and Junn 2013; Santa Ana 2002, 2013; Valentino, Brader, and Jardina 2013). The large percentage of respondents who said they had heard negative statements from media suggests that news consumption will affect perceptions of immigrant criminality.

The likely impact of news consumption on perceptions of immigrant criminality is supported by an examination of the relationship between self-reported consumption of television news and agreement with the criminal threat frames. Included in both the MSSRP and WISER polls was a question asking respondents how often they watched television news, with answers ranging from quite often to not at all on a four-point scale. In the WISER poll, whites who reported watching television news "quite often" were more likely to agree with the drugs-and-gangs statement, with 51 percent of these frequent television news viewers agreeing, compared with 35 percent of those who reported watching the news less often. Similarly, agreement that undocumented crossing was a crime and that those who did so were criminals was also related to news viewership, with 77 percent of whites who were frequent viewers agreeing, compared with 68 percent of less frequent viewers. The difference between frequent and infrequent viewers was smaller for the crossing-is-a-crime, economic-burden, and cultural threat frames in the WISER survey. In the MSSRP poll, 34 percent of frequent television news viewers believed that new immigrants increased the level of crime in the United States, compared with 28 percent of those who reported viewing the news less often, which at 6 percent was the largest difference. Table 3.2 shows the percentage difference in agreement with a given threat frame between frequent and infrequent television news viewers.

These findings suggest that news consumption may affect perceptions of criminality more than it does perceptions of the economic or cultural threat. There are two likely explanations. The first is the tendency for media stories about undocumented immigration to feature imagery that primes viewers to think of this group as criminals. As discussed earlier,

TABLE 3.2. Effect of frequent news viewing on percent agreement with MSSRP and WISER threat questions, by race

THREAT	WHITES	BLACKS
MSSRP		
Burden on housing, health care, jobs	+1	+2
Less likely to assimilate	+5	+2
Increase crime in United States	+6	+4
WISER		
Burden on housing, health care, jobs	+1	−3
Change culture for worse	+3	+5
Crossing is a crime	+9	−5
Involved with drugs and gangs	+16	+10
Increase neighborhood crime	+3	−3

the legal treatment of undocumented immigration as a crime-control issue that began with S. 5094 and the criminalization of illegal entry have resulted in many media stories featuring footage of arrests or raids. Such stories can lead viewers to perceive undocumented immigration as a crime-control issue rather than something more complex (Chiricos, Eschholz, and Gertz 1997; Chiricos, Padgett, and Gertz 2000; Doob and Macdonald 1979; Romer, Jamieson, and Aday 2003). The second likely explanation is that crime tends to get a disproportionate amount of coverage in the news media, which can lead to exaggerated fears of victimhood. Stories of immigrant criminality or claims that Mexican immigrants are associated with drug cartels can make Americans fearful of this group as a potential threat to their physical safety, in much the same way that Muslim refugees were portrayed as potential terrorists to justify the Trump administration's ban on travel from majority-Muslim countries (Merica 2017). A 2003 study by Romer, Jamieson, and Aday found that viewers of local television news were more likely to have fears of violent crime than those who did not watch local news, demonstrating the effectiveness of television news in promoting fears of victimhood (Chiricos, Eschholz, and Gertz 1997; Chiricos, Padgett, and Gertz 2000; Doob and Macdonald 1979; Romer, Jamieson, and Aday 2003). A viewer of television news who believes that undocumented immigrants are criminals appears to be more likely to have negative stereotypes and fears of the undocumented as a criminal threat. The media thus play an important role in communicating and reinforcing the immigrant-as-criminal narrative discussed in the previous chapters.

This narrative is a direct result of the legal treatment of immigrants, who with few exceptions historically have been treated as criminals, even though undocumented entry has been little more than a civil violation for most of the nation's history. Indeed, even today only the undocumented crossing of the border is an illegal act; overstaying a visa remains a civil violation. Since 2010, those overstaying their visas have accounted for the majority of undocumented immigrants in the United States, but this is not the group most envision when they think of "illegal immigrants" (Yee, Davis, and Patel 2017). S. 5094, Mexican Repatriation, Operation Wetback, and IIRIRA have all played a role in entrenching this path, as did the shortcomings of IRCA. Past policies have in turn shaped how the media cover undocumented immigration. The iconic undocumented immigrant is one who illegally crosses the border from Mexico, with that act alone marking them as a criminal both legally and in the mind of the American public. Because of the legislative treatment of this issue, this mark of criminality is borne by the immigrants alone, with the complicity of employers and the US government's own role in both creating and perpetuating the "problem" of undocumented immigration ignored in most media coverage.

The relationship between media consumption and agreement with the criminal threat frames was clearer for whites than for blacks. For whites, being a frequent consumer of television news was associated with increases in agreement across all threat frames in both studies. For blacks, on the other hand, there were some instances in which being a frequent viewer was associated with lower levels of agreement rather than higher ones (see table 3.2). In the WISER poll, blacks who reported watching television news often were less likely to agree that undocumented immigrants were a burden on the economy, that they were criminals for entering illegally, or that they increased neighborhood crime, possibly because of the disproportionate portrayal of blacks as criminals in television news, which has very likely led blacks to question how other minority groups are portrayed in the media. Past studies have found television news to have a different impact on whites' attitudes toward crime and criminals than on blacks' (Gilliam and Iyengar 2000). This could explain the different effects media coverage had on blacks and whites, though there is also the possibility that blacks and whites get their news from different outlets. This does seem to be the case, as whites in the WISER poll were more likely to be Fox News viewers, with 25 percent of whites and only 9 percent of blacks reporting that they got their news from Fox. In the same poll, blacks were more likely than whites to report getting their news from CNN, with 25 percent of blacks but only 15 percent of whites saying that CNN was their news source.

Beliefs in Immigrant Criminality among Whites

A regression analysis can isolate the effect of media consumption, while controlling for other variables that would potentially influence agreement with the criminal threat frames. To assess the impact of various independent variables on a categorical dependent variable, I used a logistic regression, which allows the effect of each independent variable to be assessed independently, while all other variables are held equal. Five logistic regressions were run, with 0 indicating disagreement with the threat frame and 1 indicating agreement. The independent variables were economic anxiety, political knowledge and feelings towards Latinos, as well as standard demographic variables such as education, age, income, and party identification. The full results appear in table A2 in the appendix.

Figure 3.2 is a ropeladder plot of the logistic regression for the criminal threat frame among white respondents, showing the coefficients for each independent variable, along with its 95 percent confidence interval. Variables whose confidence intervals do not cross the zero line are significant at the $p < .05$ level. As figure 3.2 shows, all else being equal, being a frequent consumer of television news increased the likelihood that a respondent would agree that new immigrants increased crime rates in the United States. The likelihood was also increased for individuals whose social-dominance orientation was higher, who were cooler toward Latinos, or who were male. The only variable that decreased the likelihood of agreement with this frame was making more than one hundred thousand dollars a year.

Among whites, being a frequent television news viewer was significant only for perceptions of immigrant criminality, it had no influence on agreement with any of the other frames in the MSSRP model. All else being equal, being a frequent consumer of television news increased the probability of agreeing with the criminal threat frame from 30 percent to 37 percent. Table 3.3 shows the coefficients and standard errors for the statistically significant variables in all three of the collective-threat-frame

FIGURE 3.2. Agreement with MSSRP criminal threat frame, whites only

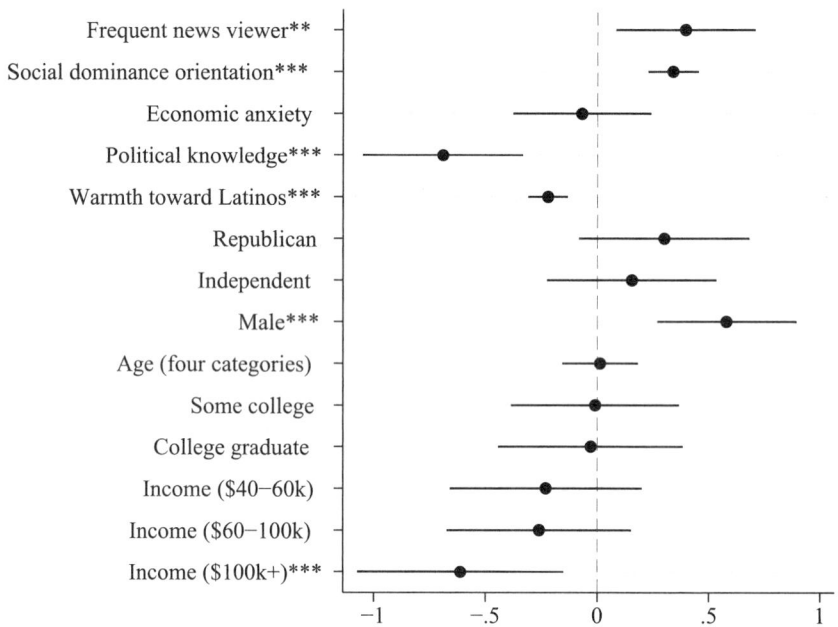

$n = 797$; *p $<$ .10; **p $<$ .05; ***p $<$ .01

models in the MSSRP poll. Being a frequent consumer of television news was the only independent variable that the criminal threat frame did not share with at least one of the other frames.

Without knowing how the frequency of television news stories about immigrant criminality compared with the frequency of those about immigrants as an economic or cultural threat, we cannot say for certain why media consumption only affects beliefs that immigrants drive up neighborhood crime rates and not that they are a drain on the American taxpayer or unassimilable. However, imagery of undocumented immigrants that suggests criminality, for example, showing them being handcuffed or arrested, is common in mainstream media, as are graphic descriptions of crimes committed by undocumented immigrants when they occur. Considering the existing evidence for the role of media in reinforcing notions of black criminality because of the exaggerated number of crime stories featuring black perpetrators, these findings suggest that the media play a similar role with regard to undocumented immigration (Entman 1994; Gilliam and Iyengar 2000; Peffley, Shields, and Williams 1996). Media

TABLE 3.3. MSSRP threat-frame models: Coefficients and standard errors for significant variables, whites only

INDEPENDENT VARIABLE	CRIMINAL THREAT	ECONOMIC THREAT	CULTURAL THREAT
Frequent news viewer	.40 (.16)**		
Social dominance	.34 (.06)***	.35 (.06)***	.29 (.05)***
Economic anxiety		.35 (.16)**	
Political knowledge	−.69 (.18)***	−.83 (.17)***	−.35 (.16)**
Warmth toward Latinos	−.22 (.04)***	−.25 (.05)***	−.22 (.05)***
Republican			.45 (.18)**
Independent		.35 (.19)*	
Male	.58 (.16)***		.30 (.15)**
Age category		−.29 (.09)***	
Some college			
College graduate		−.74 (.21)***	
Income $40,000–60,000			−.63 (.21)***
Income $60,000–100,000			−.35 (.20)*
Income $100,000+	−.61 (.24)***		−.40 (.21)*

$n = 797$; *$p < .10$; **$p < .05$; ***$p < .01$

stories about crimes by individual undocumented immigrants may create a perception that this group is predisposed to criminality, just as disproportionate coverage of black crimes reinforces stereotypes of black criminality. Like fears of victimhood from terrorism, fears of criminal immigrants are very likely tied to the sensationalism that often accompanies crimes committed by immigrants. The Steinle shooting in San Francisco, while tragic, would likely have been out of the news cycle quickly if the perpetrator had not been an undocumented immigrant and had the story not been seized upon by Donald Trump. Shootings in America are, sadly, not uncommon, with the Gun Violence Archive listing 13,496 firearm-related fatalities in 2015, the year Steinle was killed. The same kind of sensationalism and coverage is rarely afforded to questions of assimilation or whether undocumented immigrants impose an economic burden on the United States, which may explain why the amount of television news one watches has little effect on these threat frames.

Across all MSSRP models, white respondents who reported more unfavorable feelings toward Latinos than fellow whites were much more likely to agree with the criminal threat frames, revealing the racialized component to these beliefs. While the MSSRP question asked generally about threat perceptions based on "new immigration," the immigration debate in the United States is almost exclusively about undocumented immigration, and Latinos are the "iconic illegal aliens" (Ngai 2004). Warmth toward Latinos was statistically significant for all threat frames, demonstrating that attitudes toward undocumented immigrants are premised on not only their status but also their race. Similarly, social-dominance orientation was found to increase agreement with all frames. This fits with the role that social dominance has been found to play in antiblack attitudes (Pratto et al. 1994; Sidanius 1993; Sidanius and Pratto 2001). At the other end of the spectrum, those with a high level of political knowledge, measured by correct answers to three questions on US government, were less likely to agree with any of the collective-threat frames. Those with more political knowledge have been found to be less susceptible to priming effects by past research and might simply be more knowledgeable about immigration (Huber and Lapinski 2006).

Those with a high level of political knowledge were less likely to agree with the criminal threat frame even if they were frequent television news viewers. Of those who were highly knowledgeable about politics but had reported being frequent viewers of television news, 26 percent agreed with the criminal threat frame, compared with 38 percent of those with little political knowledge, revealing the moderating effect that political knowledge has on media's influence on the criminal threat frame.

While certain variables were missing from the WISER poll, notably a measure of coolness toward Latinos, social-dominance orientation, and economic anxiety, it can be used to determine whether the media effect on white beliefs in immigrant criminality can be replicated in a second poll. In the WISER poll as in the MSSRP poll, those who were more frequent consumers of television news were also more likely to express agreement with two of the three criminal threat frames. Being a frequent consumer of television news increased the likelihood of agreement with the idea that crossing was a crime and the undocumented were criminals as well as with the idea that undocumented immigrants were likely to be involved with drugs or gangs. Media consumption had no effect on whether white respondents believed that undocumented immigrants drove up neighborhood crime rates. In the case of both the MSSRP and the WISER poll, consumption of television news only had an effect on agreement with the criminal threat frames. Table 3.4 shows the coefficients and standard deviations for the statistically significant variables in the three criminal threat models from the WISER poll. The full set of

TABLE 3.4. WISER threat-frame models: Coefficients and standard errors for significant variables, whites only

INDEPENDENT VARIABLE	CROSSING IS A CRIME	DRUGS AND GANGS	INCREASE LOCAL CRIME
Frequent news viewer	.62 (.29)**	.50 (.28)*	
Republican	1.22 (.34)***	.76 (.31)**	1.12 (.33)***
Independent	.85 (.32)***	.69 (.30)**	
Male	.60 (.29)*	.79 (.25)***	.59 (.26)**
Age category	−.01 (.16)	.31 (.15)**	.33 (.15)**
Some college			
College graduate			
Income $40,000–60,000	−.79 (.36)**		
Income $60,000–100,000			
Income $100,000+			−1.03 (.55)***

$n = 292$; *$p < 10$; **$p < 05$; ***$p < 01$

logistic regression models for the WISER poll can be found in table A3 in the appendix.

Beliefs in Immigrant Criminality among Blacks

With an oversample of 355 blacks in the MSSRP poll, the models above run for white respondents can be replicated for blacks, though the party-identification variables needed to be changed since only 13 blacks identified as Republicans and 60 as independents. The majority of blacks in the study, approximately 77 percent, identified as Democrats, compared with 31 percent of whites. This isn't surprising considering that a majority of blacks in the United States tend to identify as Democrats, to the point that many consider blacks to be "electorally captured" by the Democratic Party (Frymer and Skrentny 1998). The variables for being a self-identified Republican or Independent were removed, and a dummy variable for being a Democrat was included in their stead.

Black beliefs in immigrant criminality are even more understudied than these same beliefs among whites, though the analysis earlier in this chapter found that blacks tended to agree with many of the criminal threat frames at approximately the same rates as whites. The significant variables and direction of effect for the blacks-only economic, cultural, and criminal threat frames are shown in table 3.5 and the full set of regression models is available in table A4 in the appendix.

TABLE 3.5. MSSRP threat-frame models: Coefficients and standard errors for significant variables, blacks only

INDEPENDENT VARIABLE	CRIMINAL THREAT	ECONOMIC THREAT	CULTURAL THREAT
Frequent news viewer	.55 (.32)*	.63 (.34)*	
Social dominance		.57 (.15)***	
Economic anxiety		1.51 (.39)***	1.07 (.39)***
Political knowledge			
Warmth toward Latinos			−.19 (.09)**
Democrat	−.78 (.34)**		−.71 (.34)**
Male		−.60 (.32)*	−.88 (.19)***
Some college			
College graduate		−1.09 (.53)**	
Income $40,000–60,000			
Income $60,000–100,000			
Income $100,000+			

$n = 315$; *$p < .10$; **$p < .05$; ***$p < .01$

As table 3.5 shows, there are differences between what influences whites' belief in immigrant criminality and what influences blacks'. For blacks, the only statistically significant variables were media consumption and identifying as a Democrat. Social-dominance orientation, political knowledge, and feelings toward Latinos played no role in predicting a belief that new immigrants drove up crime rates. This is intriguing considering that blacks and whites expressed a belief in immigrant criminality at approximately the same rates.

For the two other collective-threat frames in the MSSRP poll, blacks resembled whites more closely in what predicted agreement. Social-dominance orientation, political knowledge, and warmth toward Latinos were all statistically significant, and the effect was in the same direction as it was for whites. Economic anxiety did play a larger role in blacks' threat perceptions, increasing not only their perceptions of immigrants as an economic threat but also their perceptions that new immigrants did not assimilate. This finding supports studies that have shown that economics plays a large role in perceptions of competition for blacks and between minority groups more generally, which could explain the increased likelihood of seeing immigrants as an economic threat or as unwilling to adopt an American way of life (Blalock 1967; Blumer 1958; Gay 2006).

Unfortunately, the WISER poll only had an oversample of 156 blacks, and there were simply too few in the sample, along with too little variation in terms of party identification or income, to run models matching those run for whites. This meant that the models really could not provide any additional useful information concerning what influenced black perceptions of criminal threat, so they were omitted from the analysis. The rate of agreement with the criminal threat frames, the tendency of blacks to report learning these threat frames from media, and the influence the media had on perceptions of criminality all suggest that black beliefs in the immigrant-as-criminal narrative are ripe for further study.

Criminal Threat, Media, and the American Public

One thing is clear from the results of the MSSRP and WISER polls: a large number of Americans—more than 60 percent of both blacks and whites—agree that undocumented immigrants are criminals because they entered the United States illegally. This perception is a result of the racial program of criminalization in the United States, which has sought to exclude not only undocumented immigrants but Latino immigrants more generally by capitalizing on racialized anxieties about criminality (Provine and Doty 2011). S. 5094, Mexican Repatriation, Operation Wetback, increases in the Border Patrol and the INS under IRCA, and IIRIRA have all contributed to the image of the undocumented immigrant as criminal in the mind of the American public because of how the US political system treats these individuals and how political elites discuss them. Workplace and neighborhood raids, politicians advocating the building of a border wall for safety, the construction of detention centers for the undocumented, and claims that Mexican immigrants are rapists, members of drug cartels, or somehow inherently dangerous all influence how the media cover immigration and public perceptions in the United States. The overwhelmingly tendency of media to negatively characterize the undocumented through their coverage of enforcement actions, irresponsible elite rhetoric, and sensational instances of immigrant crime today influences the opinions of whites.

The acceptance that the undocumented are "criminals" justifies exclusion, fear, and harsh treatment. Already cast as outsiders in America, undocumented immigrants are also viewed as a threat to the jobs, culture, and safety of American citizens, which affects policy making on immigration. Politicians are more likely to pursue punitive policies for undocumented entry in order to appear "tough on crime" if it is clear that a significant proportion of the American public believe that it is a criminal act. Undocumented immigrants have long been seen as anticitizens who have "failed to embrace their responsibilities as subjects of the 'moral community' and must consequently be subject to permanent and despotic administration in the name of preserving the public's safety" (Inda 2008, 53). Perceptions of immigrant threat, whether cultural, economic, or criminal, help to justify draconian policies toward immigration like S. 5094 and IIRIRA and move the country further from the comprehensive immigration reform that it and its roughly eleven million undocumented immigrants so desperately need.

FOUR

Policy Preferences and the Undocumented Threat

As shown in the preceding chapter, members of the American public harbor perceptions of undocumented criminality very much in line with those espoused by members of Congress in the legislative debates over S. 5094 and IIRIRA. Legislation criminalizing the undocumented has been successful in coloring how the American public sees undocumented immigration, with a majority agreeing that it is a criminal act. Yet it is not clear what effect, if any, belief in immigrant criminality has on policy preferences. In this chapter I address this gap in knowledge by examining the role that perceived threats play in determining policy preferences on immigration. I analyze the impact that criminal, cultural, and economic threat perceptions have on four different policies to address undocumented immigration: deportation, a guest-worker program, a path to citizenship, and penalties for businesses employing the undocumented. Traditionally, solutions to undocumented immigration have ranged from deportation and felony charges to a path to citizenship, and there is a good deal of evidence for the role perceived threats play in dictating these policy preferences.

Perceived Threat and Policy Preferences

As discussed earlier, studies have found that threat perceptions can lead to increased hostility toward immigrant groups, which in turn often leads to greater support for restriction (Fetzer 2000; Stephan et al. 2005; Stephan, Ybarra, and Bachman. 1999; Wilson 2001; Zarate et al. 2004). Stephan et al. (2005) had participants read an article about Rwandan refugees that painted them as either a realistic or a symbolic threat or both. They were painted as a realistic threat because of their potential to bring violence and disease and to be a burden on the US economy. They were painted as a symbolic threat because of their different cultural and religious practices, which the article noted could clash with American values. The authors found that when Rwandans were constructed as both a symbolic and a realistic threat, attitude toward them were more negative. Wilson (2001) looked specifically at the perceived economic and cultural threats from immigrants and their impact on policy preferences. He found that opposition to policies benefitting immigrants was related to the perceived threat to the respondent. If immigrants were believed to be a threat, there was greater support for reducing immigration and less support for policies like allowing undocumented immigrants to get work permits or allowing them to attend public universities at the same cost as other students. Buckler, Swatt, and Salinas (2009) found that if undocumented immigrants are believed to pose a threat to the American economy or American culture, support for a crackdown increases. The belief that immigrants pose a threat to culture has been found to affect not only American but also European support for restriction (Buckler, Swatt, and Salinas 2009; Citrin and Sides 2008; Fetzer 2000; Wilson 2001). These studies have focused primarily on the economic and cultural frames but suggest that perceptions of criminality are also likely to play a role in policy choices, increasing the likelihood of support for deportation, for instance.

There is also a racial component to the impact of perceived threats. In a 2008 study, Brader, Valentino, and Suhay found that news stories about the costs of Mexican immigration had a different emotional effect than stories on the costs of Canadian immigration. Stories about Mexican immigrants that highlighted the threat they posed elicited more anxiety than did similar stories about Canadian immigrants. This fits with Ngai's statement that Mexicans are the "iconic" illegal immigrants and matches findings in other studies (Ngai 2004; Valentino, Brader, and Jardina 2013).

Debates over immigration laws such as Arizona's SB1070 and San Francisco's sanctuary policy frequently draw on the familiar narratives of criminal, cultural, and economic threat to justify tougher immigration laws. Elites tend to lean heavily on narratives of immigrant criminality in pushing for more restrictive policies, such as SB1070, which would have allowed police to inquire into immigration status during routine traffic stops. In 2010, Jan Brewer, in defending Senate bill 1070, pointed out time and again that undocumented immigrants were coming to the

United States not just for work but to sell drugs and terrorize families (Sanchez 2010). In 2015, Donald Trump referred to Mexican immigrants as rapists and criminals during a campaign speech and placed the blame for Kathryn Steinle's death squarely on sanctuary policies, which he claimed in a later interview "breed crime." Both claims—that Mexican immigrants are more prone to crime and that sanctuary policies increase crime rates—have been proven false by existing research (Dickey 2010; Gonzalez O'Brien, Collingwood, and El-Khatib 2017; Lyons, Velez, and Santoro 2013; Wadsworth 2010). It is thus particularly important to study the criminality frame because of its increasing use in the debate over immigration reform. To date, we have little knowledge of how this impacts policy preferences because questions about immigrant criminality are rarely asked in public-opinion surveys. What we do know, from evidence presented in chapter 3, is that perceptions of criminality seem to be unique among the threat tropes, at least in terms of media's role in influencing agreement with this frame. Past research on immigration attitudes provides evidence that negative stereotypes of immigrants affect policy preferences, suggesting that agreement with the criminality frame will have a similar effect.

Measuring Policy Preferences

To measure the effect of threat perceptions on policy preferences, participants in the WISER poll were asked four questions on immigration policy after being asked for their level of agreement with the various threat frames. Unfortunately, the MSSRP poll did not include questions on policy preferences. Responses were on a four-point Likert scale ranging from strongly agree (1) to strongly disagree (4), with no neutral category. Survey participants were asked to indicate their level of agreement with the following policies: charging all illegal immigrants as felons and sending them back to their home countries; a guest-worker program that allows immigrants to remain in the United States to work legally, but only for a time; allowing illegal immigrants already living in the United States to legally remain in the country if they have a job, pay back taxes, and learn English and eventually to become eligible for citizenship; and permanently closing down any American business or company that knowingly hires illegal immigrants.

Those who responded that they somewhat or strongly agreed were grouped together to create a dummy variable, with 1 signifying agreement and 0, disagreement. Figure 4.1 shows the level of agreement with policy among both white and black respondents. The columns add up to more than 100 percent because respondents were allowed to express agreement or disagreement with each policy.

Figure 4.1 reveals a couple of things. First, deportation and employer penalties are the least popular policies among both blacks and whites. Deportation and felony charges only received support from 33 percent of whites and 27 percent of blacks, while 44 percent of whites and 37 percent of blacks agreed with employer penalties. While the low levels of support for employer penalties are somewhat disheartening considering their necessity to comprehensive immigration reform, the findings regarding deportation were lower than expected. In contrast, in a CNN/ORC poll in 2011 more than half of respondents believed that the main focus of the government should be deportation of all undocumented immigrants in the United States (PollingReport.com 2016b).

The low level of support for deportation might be owing in part to the wording of the question, which asks not just whether undocumented immigrants should be deported but also whether they should be charged as felons. Some may not want the additional financial burden of imprisoning undocumented immigrants. It must also be noted that there was some demographic skewing in the WISER poll, with respondents being

FIGURE 4.1. Percent agreement with immigration policy options by race

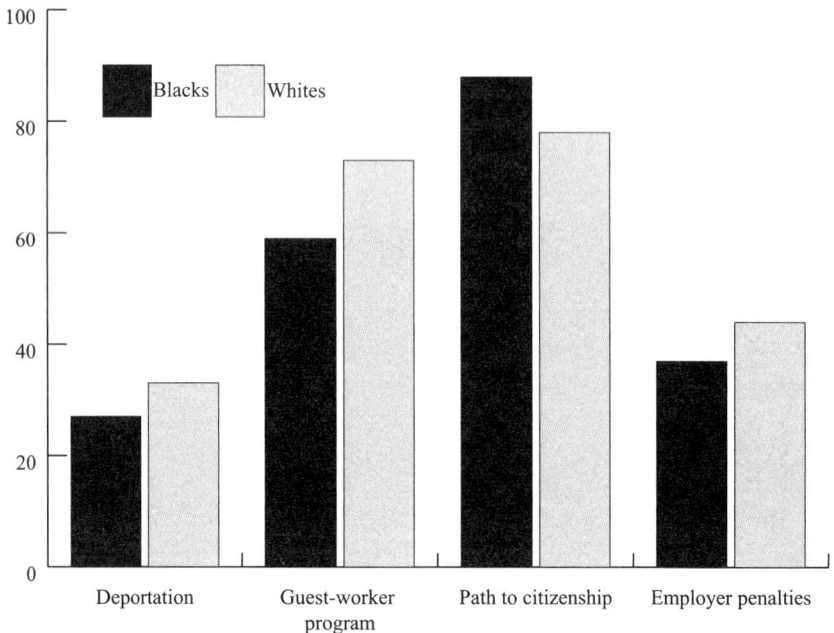

more educated and having a higher level of income than respondents to the MSSRP poll, which might have resulted in their supporting more liberal policy positions.

Second, blacks tended to express greater favorability (88%) toward a path to citizenship than did whites (78%), while whites expressed greater favorability (73%) toward a guest-worker program than did blacks (59%). It is encouraging that a majority of both blacks and whites expressed support for a path to citizenship, rather than for deportation and felony charges, with support for the latter position the least popular choice for both whites and blacks. This suggests that despite the rhetoric, there is little support for a program of mass deportation and that most Americans are in favor of more moderate policy solutions. A path to citizenship is one of the more popular solutions for undocumented immigration, with most polls since 2011 finding a majority in support of this option, though many would also like this policy to be paired with other policies, such a stricter border enforcement (PollingReport.com 2016b).

It is also useful to determine whether there were any strong correlations between any of the policy options. For whites, agreement with deportation was negatively correlated with support for a path to citizenship, though this correlation was not especially high at .20. The highest correlation was, somewhat surprisingly, between deportation and penalties for employers of undocumented immigrants, at .35. One explanation is that both support for deportation and support for employer penalties are premised on the belief that undocumented immigration is a law-and-order issue and that criminal penalties are thus the solution. Therefore, both employers and the immigrants themselves are seen as being engaged in unlawful behavior that should carry deterrent penalties. The correlation between deportation and business penalties was the strongest of any of the pairings, with most below a .10 correlation.

Among whites, party identification likely is related to support of the various policies. Self-identified Republicans are expected to be more supportive of restrictive positions like deportation and less supportive of a path to citizenship, while Democrats and Independents should be less supportive of restrictive positions and more supportive of a path to citizenship. The findings largely support expectations. Forty-four percent of white Republicans supported deportation, compared with 25 percent of Democrats and 31 percent of Independents. In addition, 52 percent of Republicans supported closing businesses that employed undocumented immigrants, compared with 42 percent of Independents and 40 percent of Democrats. Self-identified Independents were the most supportive of

FIGURE 4.2. Percent agreement with immigration policy options by party identification, whites only

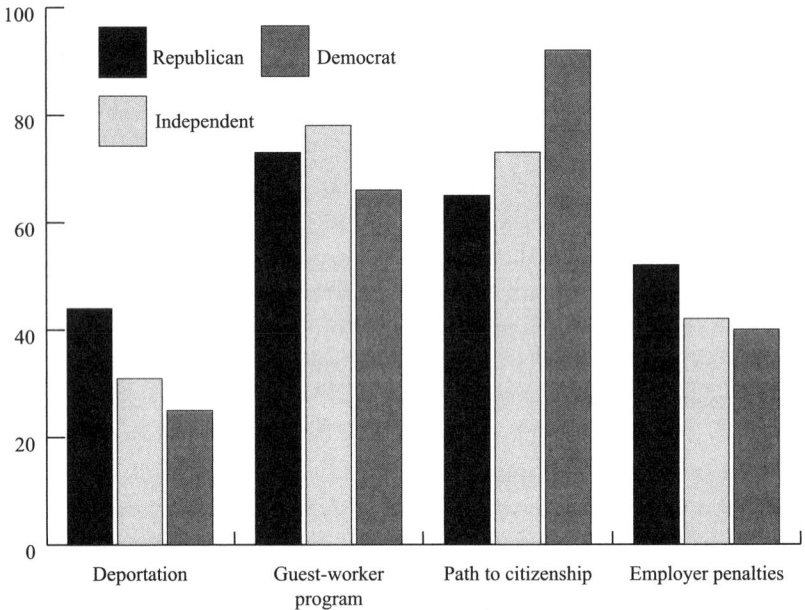

a guest-worker program, at 78 percent, but Republican support wasn't much lower at 76 percent. Among Democrats, 66 percent supported a guest-worker program. The biggest difference overall was on the question of a path to citizenship; 65 percent of Republicans supported it, compared with 91 percent of Democrats and 73 percent of Independents.

While Republicans' higher level of support for deportation and lower level of support for a path to citizenship were expected, the strong support for employer sanctions was not. Closing businesses that employed undocumented immigrants seemed to conflict with traditional GOP support for business. The expectation was a high level of support for deportation paired with a low level of support for employer sanctions, which would shift all responsibility to the immigrant, while ignoring the role of business practices in perpetuating undocumented immigration. Yet, if we think of undocumented immigration in terms of law and order, this finding makes sense. Republicans see both employer and employee as breaking the law, and therefore they see both as legitimate targets for deterrent penalties. Support for business penalties was in fact higher than support for deportation among Republican respondents. Additionally, if we go back to the congressional debate on IRCA, there were a number of Republican members of Congress who supported employer penalties. This support was premised to a large degree on narratives of law and order; for example, Representative Roukema of New Jersey acknowledged that one purpose of sanctions was to ensure that "employers are playing by the rules" (132nd Cong. Rec., 2389).

In the black oversample only a very small number self-identified as Republican; therefore, the frequencies of support vary little from those presented in figure 4.1. Black Democrats differed little from white Democrats in their support for the various policy positions, the largest difference being in support for a guest-worker program, with 66 percent of white Democrats expressing support, compared with 57 percent of blacks. The lack of a real difference between black and white Democrats suggests that policy positions are driven largely by party identification, with race playing a negligible role.

Perceived Threat and Policy Preferences

To calculate whether agreement with any of the threat frames is related to differences in support for a given policy, frequency of support of each of the four policies based on agreement with the individual threat frames was examined. To calculate the net change among those who supported each policy, the percentage of those who disagreed and supported the policy was subtracted from the percentage of those who agreed and supported it. For example, if 70 percent of those who agreed that undocumented immigrants drive up crime rates supported a path to citizenship, compared with 80 percent of those who disagreed with the frame, there would be a net change of 10 percent.

Table 4.1 reveals that perceptions that undocumented immigrants are an economic burden are associated with the largest drop in support for a path to citizenship for whites, followed by the cultural threat frame and the three criminal threat frames. A path to citizenship was the only policy option that saw a drop in support as a result of agreement, which is logical considering that it is the most "liberal" of the options on the WISER poll.

Among white respondents, the largest effect on policy preferences was a 32 percent increase in support for deportation among those who believed crossing was a crime, followed by a 22 percent increase in support for this same policy among those who thought immigrants increased neighborhood crime. There was also a 38 percent difference in support for deportation between those who believed that undocumented immigrants posed a cultural threat to the United States and those who dis-

TABLE 4.1. Effect of WISER threat-frame agreement on percent policy agreement, whites only

THREAT	DEPORTATION	GUEST-WORKER PROGRAM	PATH TO CITIZENSHIP	EMPLOYER PENALTIES
Burden on housing, health care, jobs	+30	+13	−22	+25
Change culture for worse	+38	+5	−15	+26
Crossing is a crime	+32	+16	−19	+18
Involved with drugs and gangs	+18	+8	−14	+13
Increase neighborhood crime	+22	+8	−14	+20

agreed with this frame, which was the largest difference observed for deportation preferences.

Interestingly, support for two more extreme criminal threat statements—that undocumented immigrants drive up crime rates and that they are involved with drugs and gangs—saw the smallest differences in policy preferences overall between those who agreed and disagreed. The "crossing is a crime" frame clearly had the strongest relationship to restrictive immigration policies of the three criminal threat frames. The difference in support for deportation and a path to citizenship among those who subscribed to the "crossing is a crime" frame was second overall according to the results reported in table 4.1. There was also the largest difference in support for a guest-worker program between those who agreed and disagreed with this frame, which was the highest level of agreement for any of the frames in the WISER poll, at 74 percent.

The effect that the belief in the various threat frames had on policy preferences among black respondents was also examined. Immediately apparent were some differences between whites and blacks. As table 4.2 shows, the largest difference in preferences for deportation was for those who agreed that undocumented immigrants were an economic burden on the United States. Those who agreed with this frame also agreed that undocumented immigrants should be charged with a felony and deported 41 percent more often than those who did not agree with the economic threat frame. The "drugs and gangs" frame came in second, with 21 percent more of those agreeing with the frame also supporting deportation. Overall, while the differences were smaller among blacks than among whites, those who agreed with any of the threat frames were more likely to support deportation and closing businesses that employed undocumented immigrants. The greatest difference between blacks and whites

TABLE 4.2. Effect of threat-frame agreement (WISER) on percent policy agreement, blacks only

THREAT	DEPORTATION	GUEST-WORKER PROGRAM	PATH TO CITIZENSHIP	EMPLOYER PENALTIES
Burden on housing, health care, jobs	+41	−4	−15	+25
Change culture for worse	+18	+10	−2	+15
Crossing is a crime	+18	+10	−10	+13
Involved with drugs and gangs	+17	−2	−7	+23
Increase neighborhood crime	+21	+2	−15	+8

was on the question of a guest-worker program. Among whites, agreement with any of the threat frames tended to be related to greater support for a guest-worker program, but for blacks the findings were mixed. Those who believed undocumented immigrants were an economic burden were less likely to support a guest-worker program than those who disagreed. A similar though smaller relationship was found for the "drugs and gangs" frame. This difference could be attributed to blacks being more likely to live in mixed neighborhoods with Latinos and to compete with Latino immigrants for jobs (Gay 2006; Glaeser and Vigdor 2001; Logan 2001). Thus, seeing this group as an economic burden or involved with drugs or gangs would be expected to reduce support for bringing immigrants in via a guest-worker program. Whites might see a guest-worker program as a solution to the threats presented by undocumented immigrants because presumably the government would have more control over guest workers than it does over undocumented immigrants. Since whites are less likely to compete for jobs with immigrants or to share neighborhoods with them, they may see a guest-worker program as less threatening to their economic or personal security.

Modeling White Policy Preferences and the Role of Perceived Threat

A more thorough way of examining the effects of specific threat frames on policy preferences is to use a logistic regression model to isolate the effects of the various frames on policy preferences. As in chapter 3, the dependent variable in the model, agreement with a specific policy position, is coded as a dummy variable, with 1 representing agreement. Four logistic models were used to assess the effects of the individual threat frames on policy preferences. The independent variables in the four models were the five threat frames, ranging from 1 (strong disagreement) to 4 (strong agreement); traditional demographic variables (age, gender, education, income); and party identification. Models were run separately for black and white respondents.

Table 4.3 shows the coefficients and standard errors for statistically significant variables in the four policy preference models for whites. The full models can be found in table A3 in the appendix. Beginning with a preference for deportation, a few things immediately jump out from the findings. First, of the five threat frames, three are statistically significant in predicting agreement with deportation and felony charges for undocumented immigrants among whites: that illegal entry is a criminal act, that the undocumented change American culture for the worse, and that they are an economic burden.

Of the three statistically significant threat frames, the belief that illegal entry is a crime and undocumented immigrants are criminals had the largest overall effect, increasing the predicted probability for support of deportation by 34 percent, ranging from those who strongly disagreed

TABLE 4.3. WISER policy preference models: Coefficients and standard errors for significant variables, whites only

INDEPENDENT VARIABLE	DEPORTATION	GUEST-WORKER PROGRAM	PATH TO CITIZENSHIP	EMPLOYER PENALTIES
Burden on housing, health care, jobs	.33 (.19)*			.44 (.16)**
Change culture for worse	.59 (.17)***	−.38 (.18)**		
Crossing is a crime	.75 (.23)***	.32 (.19)*	−.67 (.28)**	
Involved with drugs and gangs				
Increase neighborhood crime			−.34 (.20)*	
Republican			−1.94 (.62)***	
Independent	−.87 (.43)**		−1.64 (.62)***	
Male				
Age category				
Some college		1.54 (.48)***		
College graduate		.69 (.39)*		
Income $40,000–60,000				
Income $60,000–100,000	−.93 (.43)**			
Income $100,000+	−1.30 (.52)**	1.09 (.57)*		−.81 (.44)*

$n = 250$; *$p < .10$; **$p < .05$; ***$p < .01$

(1) to those who strongly agreed (4). The belief that undocumented immigrants changed American culture for the worse had the second largest effect. Individuals who agreed with this frame were also more likely to agree with deportation as a policy solution, with an increase in the predicted probability of 32 percent. Lastly, seeing undocumented immigrants as an economic burden increased the likelihood of support for deportation by 16 percent. The predicted probabilities for all significant variables for both the whites-only and blacks-only models can be found in table A7 in the appendix.

The effect of the "crossing is a crime" frame on preferences for deportation reveals the effectiveness of America's criminalization campaign against Latino immigrants, who because they are seen as criminals under US law are also seen as deserving of being treated as such. This despite the almost century-long reliance of the United States on undocumented labor and the role this dependency and exploitation has played in the evolution of immigration policy. While the statement that "crossing the border illegally is a crime and immigrants who come to the US this way are criminals" is factually correct because of the criminalization of undocumented entry and reentry under S. 5094, it has a significant impact on support for the most restrictive and punitive policy in the poll. This is worrying both because of the high level of agreement with the "crossing is a crime" frame (72%) and because it isn't a negative statement that can be easily refuted in the way the "drugs and gangs" or "neighborhood crime" frames can be.

This same frame also had an effect on support for a path to citizenship, leading to a 21 percent decrease in the predicted probability of support from strongly disagree (1) to strongly agree (4). The "neighborhood crime" frame was also just statistically significant at $p < .10$, with agreement leading to a 13 percent decrease in the likelihood that respondents would agree that "illegal immigrants already living in the U.S. should be allowed to legally remain in the country if they have a job, pay back taxes and learn English, and eventually become eligible for citizenship." None of the other threat frames were statistically significant for a path to citizenship, demonstrating the capability of the criminal threat frames to decrease support for liberal policies and increase support for punitive ones like deportation.

In the case of the remaining two policies, a guest-worker program and shutting down businesses found to be employing undocumented immigrants, the "crossing is a crime" frame was significant only for the former. Belief in this frame increased the probability of support for a guest-worker program by 17 percent, while the belief that the undocumented changed American culture for the worse led to a 20 percent decrease in the likelihood of support. For business penalties, only the economic threat frame was statistically significant, resulting in a 31 percent increase from strongly disagreeing to strongly agreeing.

The two more extreme criminal threat frames had no effect on preferences for any of policy options except a path to citizenship. Neither a belief that undocumented immigrants increased crime rates nor a belief that they were involved in drugs and gangs led to any real change in the likelihood of agreeing with deportation, a guest-worker program, or penalties for businesses employing undocumented immigrants. This lack of effect on deportation preferences is somewhat perplexing given that 46 percent of whites agreed with the "drugs and gangs" frame and 52 percent agreed with the "neighborhood crime" question.

Agreement with either would seem to suggest strong anti-immigrant attitudes, but this was not borne out by agreement with the policy options. Perhaps the preferred policies of those who express these beliefs simply were not represented. Perhaps they are in favor of increased border security but have much more mixed feelings toward the other policies, though this seems unlikely. As table 4.3 shows, the pattern of change for these frames is like that for the other threat tropes in that agreement drives down preferences for a path to citizenship and increases preferences for all other policies, yet only the "neighborhood crime" frame is statistically significant for reducing support for a path to citizenship. Ultimately, it is unclear why the "drugs and gangs" frame failed to have its expected effect on policy preferences.

What is clear from the white models is that a belief that undocumented entry is a crime and undocumented immigrants are therefore criminals influenced policy preferences far more than did the other threat frames. This belief increased support for deportation and a guest-worker program, while reducing the likelihood of support for a path to citizenship. While the effects of the "drugs and gangs" and "neighborhood crime" frames were not as strong as expected, it is clear that perceptions of immigrant criminality strongly influence white policy preferences for undocumented immigration.

Of the demographic variables in the model, being a self-identified Independent and earning from $60,000 to more than $100,000 annually decreased one's support for deportation charges. For a guest-worker program, having completed some college or being a college graduate and earning more than $100,000 a year increased support. Other than the two criminal threat frames, the only other significant variables affecting support to a path to citizenship were being a Republican and being an Independent, both of which reduced support for this policy. Lastly, for business penalties, those earning more than $100,000 a year were less likely to support closing businesses that employed undocumented immigrants.

These findings support the argument that criminalization of undocumented entry has had an important impact on public opinion and policy preferences. White respondents overwhelmingly agreed that the undocumented are criminals because of how they entered and thus tended to support attaching criminal penalties to this behavior.

Modeling Black Policy Preferences and the Role of Perceived Threat

A similar set of models was run for the black oversample, though some changes were necessary because of the size of the oversample. Of the 155 black respondents in the WISER poll, there were simply not enough in each income category to allow the same dummy variables to be used as in the whites-only models. Therefore, a dummy variable was created for all those earning $40,000 or more annually, which was roughly half of those who responded to the income question. There was a similar problem with party identification, with only 4 blacks self-identifying as Republicans and 29 as Independents. The dummy variable for those identifying as Democrats, who made up most of the sample, was used instead of including dummy variables for Republicans and Independents, who were omitted as the comparison category.

Unfortunately, because of the small sample size and the high level of support for a path to citizenship among blacks, there were not enough observations to run a model for this policy option. Among blacks respondents, 137 of 155, or 88 percent, supported a path to citizenship for undocumented immigrants, compared with 78 percent of the larger white sample. This lack of variety in policy preferences among blacks made it impossible to run a regression model. The coefficients and standard errors for the statistically significant variables for the deportation, guest-worker, and business-penalties models are reported in table 4.4, and the full models can be found in table A6 in the appendix.

For blacks, the only significant variable for deportation preferences was a perception of economic threat. None of the other threat frames met the $p < .10$ threshold, usually used to denote statistical significance in political science. A belief that undocumented immigrants were an eco-

TABLE 4.4. WISER policy preference models: Coefficients and standard errors for significant variables, blacks only

INDEPENDENT VARIABLE	DEPORTATION	GUEST-WORKER PROGRAM	PATH TO CITIZENSHIP
Burden on housing, health care, jobs	1.51 (.41)***		.60 (.28)**
Change culture for worse			
Crossing is a crime			
Involved with drugs and gangs			
Increase neighborhood crime			
Democrat			
Male		−.83 (.48)*	
Age category			
Some college			
College graduate	1.34 (.77)*		1.31 (.60)**
Income $40,000+	−1.19 (.71)*	.97 (.50)*	

$n = 106$; *$p < 10$; **$p < .05$; ***$p < .01$

nomic burden increased the predicted probability that a black respondent would agree with deportation by 61 percent, ranging from the lowest level of agreement (strongly disagree) to the highest (strongly agree). Table A7 in the appendix shows the predicted probability for both black and white models. This was one of the largest effects for any variable in either the black or the white model. Being a college graduate increased support for deportation among blacks, while those making more than $40,000 a year were less supportive.

Some researchers have argued that because many blacks live near or compete with Latino immigrants for work, they are more likely to see Latino immigrants generally as a threat (Alozie and Ramirez 1999; Betancur and Gills 2000; Kerr, Miller, and Reid 2000). They further suggest that perceptions of economic threat or burden also influence preferences for the most restrictive of immigration stances, more so among blacks than among whites.

None of the threat frames were statistically significant for support among blacks for a guest-worker program, though the "drugs and gangs" frame was just shy of statistical significance, at .108. This seems to suggest that with a larger sample this frame could reach statistical significance. Outside of being male, which reduced support for a guest-worker program, or making more than $40,000 a year, which increased it, no other variables were significant for this model.

For the final option, the closure of businesses found employing undocumented immigrants, only the economic threat frame was significant. Believing that the undocumented imposed an economic burden on the United States increased support for closing those businesses employing them illegally. Agreement with this frame increased the predicted probability of support for employer penalties by 36 percent among blacks, from strongly disagree (1) to strongly agree (4). The only other variable that affected agreement with this option was being a college graduate, which increased the likelihood of support.

The criminality frames, all else being equal, do increase support for deportation among whites but not among blacks. All threat frames have a statistically significant effect in one of the models apart from the "drugs and gangs" frame, which did not achieve statistical significance in any of the models. For whites, the "crossing is a crime" frame was the most influential. It had the greatest effect overall on preferences for deportation, support for a guest-worker program, and opposition to a path to citizenship for undocumented immigrants. For blacks, the most effective frame by far was that undocumented immigrants were an economic burden, which increased support for deportation and business penalties.

This is obviously an area ripe for further research, as perceptions of criminality clearly affect policy preferences, though the effects varied based on how this criminality was framed. Future studies should include more policy options in order to discover whether either the "drugs and gangs" or the "crime rates" frame influences support for things like building a border wall, ICE raids, or an increase in the size of the Border Patrol.

Criminality and Policy Preferences

The findings discussed above suggest that belief in immigrant criminality, arising from the legislative criminalization of undocumented entry by S. 5094, has affected white Americans' policy preferences. This framing of immigrant criminality did not affect the policy preferences of blacks in this survey, however. The only threat frame that seemed to affect black respondents was the perception of economic threat. The probability of supporting deportation or closing businesses that employed undocumented immigrants increased according to the level of agreement with this frame.

Whites who subscribe to a belief that undocumented immigrants are criminals are more supportive of deportation and less supportive of a path to citizenship, revealing the continuing influence of S. 5094 and IIRIRA. The legal criminalization of undocumented immigration has led to its framing as a crime-control issue, leading to a large number of Americans today believing the immigrant-as-criminal narrative. This perceived connection between the undocumented and criminality continues to influence how people think about undocumented immigration and its solutions. America has tried charging undocumented immigrants with felonies and deporting them since 1929; and except during periods of significantly increased activity, such as during Mexican Repatriation or Operation Wetback, it has failed to have much of an impact on undocumented immigration. To continue down this same path ignores how completely it has failed, as well as the very human costs it has wrought.

There were some bright spots in the data that should be highlighted. Despite the level of agreement with the "crossing is a crime" frame, the most popular option by far in the study was a path to citizenship. In the WISER poll, 78 percent of whites and 88 percent of blacks supported a path to citizenship. Even among those who strongly agreed with the "crossing is a crime" frame, 62 percent of whites and 82 percent of blacks agreed that a path to citizenship should be one of the solutions to undocumented immigration. Among those who strongly disagreed with this frame, 93 percent of whites and 95 percent of blacks were in support of the most liberal option in the survey. While the effect of perceptions of criminal threat are worth noting, it is also important to note that a majority of Americans, black or white, support a compassionate solution for undocumented immigrants in the United States.

Criminalization and Reform

The convergence between immigration and crime began much earlier in the nation's history than is typically noted. The culmination of a period of increasing hostility to Mexican immigrants that had begun in 1924 with the formation of the Border Patrol, Senate bill 5094, also known as the Undesirable Aliens Act, helped to set the United States on a path where undocumented immigration would be handled as a crime-control issue, with a focus on border militarization and the apprehension of undocumented workers. By attaching criminal penalties to the act of undocumented entry, S. 5094 created a legal linkage between immigration and crime that previously had been largely rhetorical. From the nation's founding, there had been a suspicion of the foreign born and a tendency to attribute greater criminality to this group, but with Mexican immigrants this linkage would be legally formalized. In the post–World War I period, borders would harden, and the tradition of Mexican immigration being simply a function of labor demands would come to an end. S. 5094 criminalized undocumented immigration, making Mexican immigrants for the first time "illegal" as the term is understood today.

The Bracero Program in 1942 tried to guarantee access to undocumented labor through a guest-worker program for those who wished to come to the United States to work, but it did little to address undocumented immigration, which many employers continued to rely upon despite the Bracero Program. Those who had already entered illegally, as well as those who entered illegally despite the Bracero Program, were still seen and treated as criminals. It was not the character of the immigrants nor their contributions to the nation that mattered, but simply whether they had submitted to inspection and entered the United States legally. This would lead to the 1954 mass-deportation program known as Operation Wetback, which was evidence of how entrenched criminalization had become in immigration enforcement. The goal of this program was the forced removal of one million undocumented immigrants through aggressive apprehension and deportation. Over the course of Operation Wetback, many lost their lives due to poor conditions in their means of transportation back to Mexico. Mae Ngai (2004) compared the ships used to transport some to eighteenth-century slave ships and wrote that others died as a result of being dropped in the desert, far from either water or shade. These human costs of America's campaign of criminalization continue today, with immigrants losing their lives trying to cross areas that are increasingly inhospitable because of the militarization of the southern border, something all too frequently ignored in elite discourse or media coverage of undocumented immigration.

For fifty-seven years following passage of S. 5094, there was no congressional attempt to comprehensively address undocumented immigration; interventions were instead piecemeal attempts to either ensure access to labor (the Bracero Program) or forcibly remove the undocumented (Operation Wetback). Despite the reliance of the United States on Mexican laborers, including undocumented laborers, not until 1986 was a comprehensive approach even attempted. This attempt was the result of a moment of punctuated equilibrium created by the election of a president in favor of open borders, a growing undocumented population, a divided Congress, and an increasingly frustrated American public who throughout the 1970s and 1980s had become more aware of undocumented immigration as an issue.

While IRCA increased the size of the Border Patrol, border security was paired for the first time with an amnesty program, employer sanctions, and a guest-worker program in an attempt at a more holistic approach to the issue than had been attempted in the past. This new approach was reflected in differences in the way undocumented immigration was framed in Johnson-Reed, S. 5094, and IRCA. Debate over Johnson-Reed and S. 5094 was largely negative when it came to Mexican immigrants, with the criminality frame being relied upon regularly to push for stricter restrictions, either by including Mexico in national quotas (Johnson-Reed) or by criminalizing entry or reentry (S. 5094). In contrast, while most of the frames referenced in IRCA were still negative, there were far more positive framings of undocumented immigrants. More members of

Congress spoke of the undocumented as economic contributors, family oriented, and in pursuit of the same dream that had brought other immigrants to this country. This new rhetoric reflected the shift in policy away from an almost exclusive focus on enforcement to a multipronged attempt to overhaul the relationship between the United States and both its undocumented population and the laborers from Mexico and Central America that it relied upon.

Unfortunately, IRCA turned out to be a critical policy failure and helped to reinforce the previously existing path of US immigration policy, which treated undocumented immigration not as a labor issue but instead as a law-and-order issue, with an almost singular focus on punitive methods of control. Critical policy failures, as explained in the introduction, are policies that attempt a significant shift in how problems are addressed but come to be seen as failures because of their shortcomings. This leads to a return to the previous approach to the problem and can reinforce the earlier preferred policy path, in this case criminalization. When IRCA's pivot away from enforcement came up short, when the guest-worker program, increase in the Border Patrol, and employer sanctions failed to have their intended effect of slowing undocumented immigration, the United States returned to the path of criminalization.

The Illegal Immigration Reform and Immigrant Responsibility Act of 1996 reintroduced the rhetoric of old, with an emphasis on nativist characterizations of the undocumented population as a threat to Americans. The IIRIRA debate focused on the supposed role of immigrants in drug smuggling, theft, gang activity, and even murder despite evidence to the contrary. IIRIRA was a return to what was politically safe, what Jonathan Simon calls "governing through crime" (J. Simon 2001). Undocumented immigrants were lumped in with criminals so that politicians could justify a one-dimensional but ultimately politically convenient response—criminalization. The solution was easy: more Border Control, more INS (and later ICE), more raids, more deportations, all of which, even if they did little to truly address undocumented immigration, could be sold as being essentially "tough on crime." Never mind that in the fifty-seven years between passage of S. 5094 and IRCA these methods proved to be ineffectual at reducing undocumented immigration or the US reliance on undocumented labor. The politics of nativism and racism were embraced once again, and the angry rhetoric that characterized undocumented immigration as a matter of personal responsibility, as a decision to deliberately flaunt the laws of the United States, returned.

This return to the criminalization of the undocumented of course ignored what had been highlighted in the IRCA debate: the role of employers. As early as 1924, agricultural interests had defended their access to undocumented labor, while the immigrants were scapegoated for working for low wages and in poor conditions, for coming in search of a better life and a way to help their families. Until the passage of IRCA, the US Congress had looked the other way when American companies often deliberately violated the law to increase profits. IRCA changed this, briefly. In the IRCA debate, employers were criticized frequently and their role was emphasized. Unfortunately, IRCA's great ambition to overhaul US immigration policy by discouraging the hiring of undocumented immigrants and the creation of a guest-worker program for legal access to Mexican labor ultimately came up short. Instead of reflecting on IRCA as good policy, as a step toward comprehensively addressing undocumented immigration, many now view it as having done little more than reward illegal behavior through its amnesty program, while also insulting all those who had immigrated legally.

The intertwining of immigration and crime has long been part and parcel of elite rhetoric and US policy. Path dependence and the appeal of simple approaches to complex problems suggest that it will be very hard to break out of this cycle. Yet, the convergence of factors that occurred in the 1980s, creating a moment of punctuated equilibrium in which real change in immigration policy was possible, could happen again. Recognizing these windows of opportunity will give reformers a better shot at immigration policy that is truly comprehensive and not simply focused on restriction and criminalization.

In these moments of punctuated equilibrium, public opinion, and the elevation of immigration onto the policy agenda that often results from greater public awareness and concern, is important. We could be close to one of those moments, as the divisive rhetoric of the Trump administration reveals the racism and xenophobia that have long simmered under the surface of US immigration policy. What remains to be seen is whether this alternate vision can be realized in a political environment in which the president campaigned on the creation of a deportation force modeled on Operation Wetback and a wall between the United States and Mexico, regularly using graphic descriptions of immigrant criminality to justify these policies.

Unfortunately, comprehensive reform faces significant hurdles, not the least of which is the belief of many Americans that undocumented immigrants are criminals. More than 60 percent of both blacks and whites agreed that undocumented crossing is a crime and that unauthorized immigrants are criminals, revealing just how deeply this frame has penetrated the American psyche. Though the other two criminal threat frames had lower levels of agreement, approximately 40 percent of both blacks and whites agreed that undocumented immigrants are involved with drugs and gangs, while 52 percent of whites and roughly 36 percent of blacks agreed that they increase neighborhood crime rates. These findings are troubling, to say the least. For comprehensive immigration reform to become a reality, Americans must trust that at least a good number of the approximately eleven million undocumented immigrants currently in the United States are law abiding, hardworking, and non-threatening. If they believe these individuals are criminals, legalization will be resisted and comprehensive reform will be stymied, since it can only be achieved with some kind of path to citizenship for those already in the United States.

The media must play a role in helping to change public opinion, and immigration advocates must find creative ways to use the media to push for reform instead of restriction. Most Americans reported that they heard immigrant threat frames from some media source, and the models revealed that all else being equal, news consumption increased perceptions of criminal threat, at least among white Americans. The media's obsession with crime is really nothing new, but like blacks, undocumented immigrants are disproportionately portrayed in ways that suggest criminality and danger. These portrayals have a significant effect on attitudes toward the undocumented population and perceptions that this group is predisposed to criminality. In the right-wing sound bites about headless bodies, rape, and kidnappings we can see the echoes of Ronald Reagan's talk of welfare queens and crack babies, both scare campaigns aimed at tapping into nativist or racist tendencies in the American public. Media are the conduit through which these messages reach the public, and it is clear that they have their intended effect. Since frequent consumers of television news are more likely to believe that undocumented immigrants are criminals, advocates of compassionate immigration reform must find a way to address the narratives and imagery of immigrant criminality that are so common in the media.

While more Americans believe this narrative than would be desired, most Americans do not believe that undocumented immigrants drive up crime rates or are involved in drugs and gangs. Optimism can also be drawn from the finding that most Americans support a path to citizenship or a guest-worker program, with a minority in support of deportation and felony charges. Notions of immigrant criminality did influence these preferences, though, and a belief that undocumented crossing is a crime increased support for deportation and reduced support for a path to citizenship. This pernicious effect of legal criminalization will continue to reverberate for the foreseeable future because it has been part of US immigration policy for so long. Findings in chapter 4 suggest that perceptions of criminality help to drive further criminalization by increasing support for restrictive policies that treat undocumented immigration as a crime, which in turn influence which solutions politicians see as viable. Counternarratives must be developed that focus on what is supported by study after study: that undocumented immigrants are not criminals and often offend at rates lower than the native-born population. This message must be aggressively promoted, and the decriminalization of undocumented entry and comprehensive reform just as aggressively pursued. It will take decades, if not longer, to erase the stereotypes associated with undocumented immigrants because of America's history of immigration policy.

The findings of this book suggest many valuable paths for future research, the most important being research on public opinion toward immigrant criminality. In future studies, positively valanced frames should be included to determine whether the American public believes, for instance, that undocumented immigrants are law abiding or less likely to be involved in crime. In addition, survey experiments could be used to analyze counternarratives to the criminal threat frame. Does, for instance, citing figures showing low offense rates have any impact on policy preferences? How can perceptions of criminality be challenged in a way that results not in a backlash effect but instead in actual attitude change?

The polls drawn on for this study had some limitations. The WISER poll, which I relied on for an analysis of policy preferences, had a small sample size. Larger national studies would allow examination of geographic effects, as well of proximity. Does living close to a large Latino community have any effect on perceptions of criminality? Future work could also include a wider range of policy options than were available here, perhaps especially increasing the size of the Border Patrol and security on the border. Including these as options could also help explain why a belief that undocumented immigrants increased crime rates had no effect on policy preferences for either blacks or whites.

The criminalization of undocumented immigration remains an understudied area, though the literature at least on the policy side is growing. However, often ignored is the path dependence that has resulted from legislation like S. 5094 and IIRIRA, which have helped to entrench immigration as a law-and-order issue. The criminalization of undocumented immigration needs to be interrogated further. This book is meant as a starting point. There is much more work to be done.

FIGURE A1. Undocumented population in the United States, 1974–2010

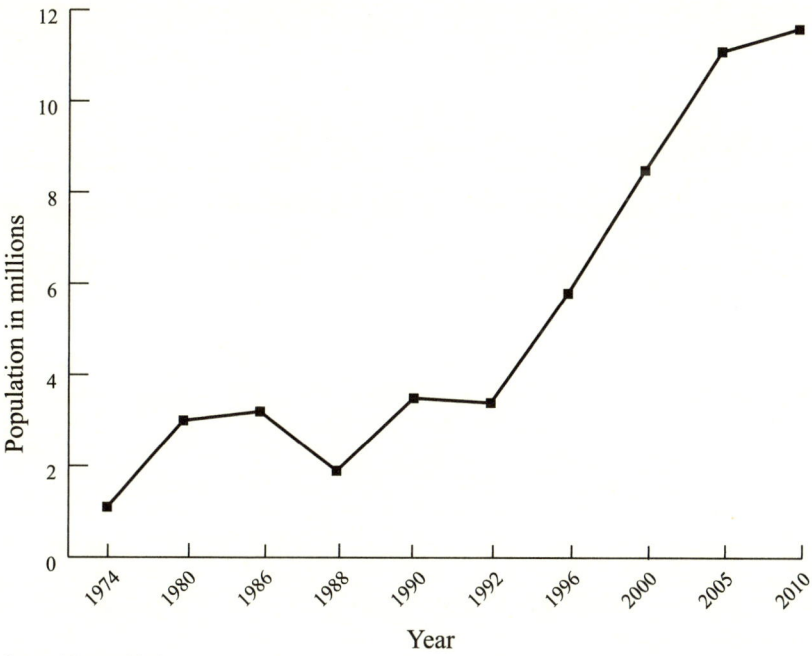

Source: Wasem 2012

TABLE A1. Descriptive statistics, WISER poll (%)

VARIABLE	WHITES	BLACKS
Age 18–34	10	14
Age 35–54	30	26
Age 55–74	42	43
Age 75+	17	17
Male	60	59
Democrat	35	75
Independent	32	19
Republican	29	3
High school	22	33
Some college	24	29
College graduate	54	37
Postgraduate	20	13
Income less than $40,000	24	36
Income $40,000–60,000	17	10
Income $60,000–100,000	22	22
Income $100,000+	15	6

TABLE A2. MSSRP threat-frame models, whites only

INDEPENDENT VARIABLE	CRIMINAL THREAT	ECONOMIC THREAT	CULTURAL THREAT
Frequent news viewer	.40 (.16)**	−.07 (.16)	.15 (.15)
Social dominance	.34 (.06)***	.35 (.06)***	.29 (.05)***
Economic anxiety	−.07 (.16)	.35 (.16)**	.18 (.15)
Political knowledge	−.69 (.18)***	−.83 (.17)***	−.35 (.16)**
Warmth toward Latinos	−.22 (.04)***	−.25 (.05)***	−.22 (.05)***
Republican	.30 (.19)	.13 (.19)	.45 (.18)**
Independent	.15 (.19)	.35 (.19)*	.18 (.18)
Male	.58 (.16)***	.19 (.16)	.30 (.15)**
Age category	.01 (.09)	−.29 (.09)***	−.09 (.08)
Some college	−.01 (.19)	−.13 (.19)	−.04 (.18)
College graduate	−.03 (.21)	−.74 (.21)***	.28 (.20)
Income $40,000–60,000	−.23 (.22)	−.13 (.21)	−.63 (.21)***
Income $60,000–100,000	−.26 (.21)	−.03 (.21)	−.35 (.20)*
Income $100,000+	−.61 (.24)***	−.29 (.23)	−.40 (.21)*

$n = 797$; *$p < .10$; **$p < .05$; ***$p < .01$

TABLE A3. WISER threat-frame models, whites only

INDEPENDENT VARIABLE	CROSSING IS A CRIME	DRUGS AND GANGS	INCREASE LOCAL CRIME
Frequent news viewer	.62 (.29)**	.50 (.28)*	−.19 (.28)
Republican	1.22 (.34)***	.76 (.31)**	1.12 (.33)***
Independent	.85 (.32)***	.69 (.30)**	.12 (.30)
Male	.60 (.29)*	.79 (.25)***	.59 (.26)**
Age category	−.01 (.16)	.31 (.15)**	.33 (.15)**
Some college	−.12 (.39)	−.26 (.35)	.07 (.38)
College graduate	−.04 (.35)	−.53 (.32)	.12 (.34)
Income $40,000–60,000	−.79 (.36)**	−.03 (.35)	−.10 (.37)
Income $60,000–100,000	.23 (.37)	.35 (.32)	.43 (.34)
Income $100,000+	.14 (.59)	−.25 (.38)	−1.03 (.55)***

$n = 292$; *$p < 10$; **$p < 05$; ***$p < 01$

TABLE A4. MSSRP threat-frame models, blacks only

INDEPENDENT VARIABLE	CRIMINAL THREAT	ECONOMIC THREAT	CULTURAL THREAT
Frequent news viewer	.55 (.32)*	.63 (.34)*	.44 (.32)
Social dominance	.11 (.13)	.57 (.15)***	−.12 (.13)
Economic anxiety	.57 (.38)	1.51 (.39)***	1.07 (.39)***
Political knowledge	−.45 (.48)	.17 (.46)	−.08 (.42)
Warmth toward Latinos	.08 (.09)	.04 (.09)	−.19 (.09)**
Democrat	−.78 (.34)**	−.00 (.36)	−.71 (.34)**
Male	−.15 (.31)	−.60 (.32)*	−.88 (.19)***
Some college	−.13 (.36)	−.23 (.37)	−.33 (.36)
College graduate	−.55 (.52)	−1.09 (.53)**	−.10 (.47)
Income $40,000–60,000	−.71 (.49)	.11 (.45)	.35 (.44)
Income $60,000–100,000	−.40 (.47)	−.43 (.47)	.48 (.46)
Income $100,000+	−.43 (.66)	−.69 (.66)	.32 (.58)

$n = 315$

TABLE A5. WISER policy-preference models, whites only

INDEPENDENT VARIABLE	DEPORTATION	GUEST-WORKER PROGRAM	PATH TO CITIZENSHIP	EMPLOYER PENALTIES
Burden on housing, health care, jobs	.33 (.19)*	.13 (.19)	−.35 (.22)	.44 (.16)**
Change culture for worse	.59 (.17)***	−.38 (.18)**	.01 (.18)	.24 (.16)
Crossing is a crime	.75 (.23)***	.32 (.19)*	−.67 (.28)**	.11 (.17)
Involved with drugs and gangs	−.06 (.18)	.21 (.18)	.17 (.20)	−.04 (.16)
Increase neighborhood crime	.13 (.18)	.02 (.18)*	−.34 (.20)	.08 (.16)
Republican	−.61 (.44)	.28 (.43)	1.94 (.62)***	.00 (.38)
Independent	−.87 (.43)**	.00 (.39)	1.64 (.62)***	−.33 (.36)
Male	.05 (.34)	−.52 (.33)	.05 (.37)	.26 (.30)
Age category	−.22 (.19)	−.06 (.17)	−.18 (.22)	−.18 (.16)
Some college	.27 (.48)	1.54 (.48)***	.65 (.55)	−.00 (.41)
College graduate	.30 (.44)	.69 (.39)*	−.18 (.47)	−.56 (.37)
Income $40,000–60,000	−.10 (.51)	.72 (.48)	−.44 (.59)	.34 (.43)
Income $60,000–100,000	−.93 (.43)**	−.16 (.40)	−.22 (.47)	.18 (.37)
Income $100,000+	−1.30 (.52)**	1.09 (.57)*	−.09 (.53)	−.81 (.44)*

$n = 250$; *$p < .10$; **$p < .05$; ***$p < .01$

TABLE A6. WISER policy-preference models, blacks only

INDEPENDENT VARIABLE	DEPORTATION	GUEST-WORKER PROGRAM	EMPLOYER PENALTIES
Burden on housing, health care, jobs	1.51 (.41)***	−.35 (.27)	.60 (.28)**
Change culture for worse	.15 (.36)	.32 (.29)	.15 (.36)
Crossing is a crime	.06 (.37)	.30 (.22)	.06 (.37)
Involved with drugs and gangs	−.32 (.37)	−.45 (.28)	−.31 (.37)
Increase neighborhood crime	.17 (.42)	.41 (.31)	.17 (.42)
Democrat	−.62 (.69)	−.13 (.52)	−.62 (.69)
Male	−.09 (.63)	−.83 (.48)*	−.09 (.63)
Age category	−.12 (.32)	.22 (.26)	−.12 (.32)
Some college	.27 (.79)	−.37 (.60)	.27 (.79)
College graduate	1.34 (.77)*	−.35 (.57)	1.31 (.60)**
Income $40,000+	−1.19 (.71)*	.97 (.50)*	−.37 (.51)

$n = 106$; *$p < .10$; **$p < .05$; ***$p < .01$

TABLE A7. WISER percent change in predicted probability for significant variables

INDEPENDENT VARIABLE	DEPORTATION	GUEST-WORKER PROGRAM	PATH TO CITIZENSHIP	EMPLOYER PENALTIES
WHITES ONLY				
Burden on housing, health care, jobs	+16		−18	+13
Change culture for worse	+22	−12		+25
Crossing is a crime	+24			
Republican			−27	
Independent	−13		−20	
Male				
Age category				
Some college		+22		
College graduate		+11		
Income $40,000–60,000				
Income $60,000–100,000	−15			
Income $100,000+	−19	+15		−17
BLACKS ONLY				
Burden on housing, health care, jobs	+60			+35
Change culture for worse	+22	−12		+25
Crossing is a crime	+24			
Democrat				
Male		−15		
Age category				
Some college				
College graduate	+15			+25
Income $40,000+	−14	+19		

BIBLIOGRAPHY

Abrajano, M., and S. Singh. 2009. "Examining the Link between Issue Attitudes and News Source: The Case of Latinos and Immigration Reform." *Political Behavior* 31:1–30.

Akdenizli, B., E. J. Dionne, M. Kaplan, T. Rosensteil, and R. Suro. 2008. *Media and the Immigration Debate*. Washington, DC: Brookings Institute.

Alexander, M. 2010. *The New Jim Crow: Mass Incarceration in the Age of Color-Blindness*. New York: New Press.

Alozie, N., and E. Ramirez. 1999. "A Piece of the Pie and More Competition and Hispanic Employment on Urban Police Forces." *Urban Affairs Review* 34 (3): 456–75.

Baker, S. G. 1990. *The Cautious Welcome: The Legalization Programs of the Immigration Reform and Control Act*. Santa Monica, CA: RAND Corporation; Washington, DC: Urban Institute Press.

Balderrama, F. 1995. *Decade of Betrayal: Mexican Repatriation in the 1930s*. Albuquerque: University of New Mexico Press.

Baumgartner, F. R., and B. D. Jones. 1993. *Agendas and Instability in American Politics*. Chicago: University of Chicago Press.

Beinart, P. 2015. "Hillary Clinton and the Tragic Politics of Crime." *Atlantic*, 1 May. http://www.theatlantic.com/politics/archive/2015/05/the-tragic-politics-of-crime/392114/.

Betancur, J., and D. Gills, eds. 2000. *The Collaborative City: Opportunities and Struggles for Blacks and Latinos in U.S. Cities*. New York: Garland.

Blalock, H. M. 1967. *Toward a Theory of Minority-Group Relations*. New York: Wiley.

Blumer, H. 1958. "Race Prejudice as a Sense of Group Position." *Pacific Sociological Review* 1 (1): 3–7.

Bobo, L. 1983. "Whites' Opposition to Busing: Symbolic Racism or Realistic Group Conflict?" *Journal of Personality and Social Psychology* 45 (6): 1196–1210.

————. 1988. "Group Conflict, Prejudice, and the Paradox of Contemporary Racial Attitudes." In *Eliminating Racism: Profiles in Controversy,* ed. P. A. Katz and D. A. Taylor, 85–114. New York: Plenum.

————. 1999. "Prejudice as Group Position: Microfoundations of a Sociological Approach to Racism and Race Relations." *Journal of Social Issues* 55 (3): 445–72.

Bobo, L., and V. Hutchings. 1996. "Perceptions of Racial Group Competition: Extending Blumer's Theory of Group Position to a Multiracial Social Context." *American Sociological Review* 61 (6): 951–72.

Brader, T., N. A. Valentino, and E. Suhay. 2008. "What Triggers Public Opposition to Immigration? Anxiety, Group Cues, and Immigration Threat." *American Journal of Political Science* 52 (4): 959–78.

Branton, R., E. C. Cassese, B. S. Jones, and C. Westerland. 2011. "All along the Watchtower: Acculturation Fear, Anti-Latino Affect, and Immigration." *Journal of Politics* 73 (3): 664–79.

Branton, R. , and J. Dunaway. 2009. "Spatial Proximity to the US-Mexico Border and Newspaper Coverage of Immigration Issues." *Political Research Quarterly* 62 (2): 289–302.

Breitigam, G. 1920. "Welcomed Mexican Invasion." *New York Times,* 20 June.

Brimelow, P. 1996. *Alien Nation: Common Sense about America's Immigration Disaster.* New York: Harper Perennial.

Buckler, K., M. L. Swatt, and P. Salinas. 2009. "Public Views of Illegal Immigration Policy and Control Strategies: A Test of Core Hypotheses." *Journal of Criminal Justice* 37: 317–27.

California Proposition 187. 1994. https://repository.uchastings.edu/ca_ballot _props/1104/.

Certificates of Arrival, Naturalization Law Amendments, Etc: Hearings before the Committee on Immigration and Naturalization, House of Representatives. 1929. 70th Congress.

Chavez, L. R. 2008. *The Latino Threat: Constructing Immigrants, Citizens, and the Nation.* Stanford, CA: Stanford University Press.

Chavez, M., S. Whiteford, and J. Hoewe. 2010. "Reporting on Immigration: A Content Analysis of Major US Newspapers' Coverage of Mexican Immigration." *Norteamérica* 5 (2): 111–25.

Chiricos, T., S. Eschholz, and M. Gertz. 1997. "Crime, News and Fear of Crime: Toward an Identification of Audience Effects." *Social Problems* 44 (3): 342–57.

Chiricos, T., K. Padgett, and M. Gertz. 2000. "Fear, TV News, and the Reality of Crime." *Criminology* 38 (3): 755–86.

Chishti, M., and C. Kamasaki. 2014. "IRCA in Retrospect: Guideposts for Today's Immigration Reform." *Migration Policy Institution Policy Brief,* no. 9 (January).

Chishti, M., D. Meissner, and C. Bergeron. 2011. "At Its 25th Anniversary, IRCA's Legacy Lives On." *Online Journal of the Migration Policy Institute,* 16 November. https://www.migrationpolicy.org/article/its-25th-anniversary-ircas-legacy -lives.

Citrin, J., and J. Sides. 2008. "Immigration and the Imagined Community in Europe and the United States." *Political Studies* 56 (1): 33–56.

Clark, N. H. 1976. *Deliver Us from Evil: An Interpretation of American Prohibition.* New York: Norton.

Cohen, J. 1931. "Report on Crime and the Foreign Born: Comment." *Michigan Law Review* 30 (1): 99–104.

Cooper, B., and K. O'Neil. 2005. "Lessons from the Immigration Reform and Control Act of 1986." Migration Policy Institute Policy Brief, no. 3 (August). https://www.migrationpolicy.org/research/lessons-immigration-reform-and -control-act-1986.

C-SPAN. 1980. *Republican Presidential Candidates Debate.* https://www.c-span.org /video/?407380-1/1980-republican-presidential-candidates-debate.

Dickey, C. 2010. "How Immigrants Actually Reduce Crime." *Newsweek,* 26 May. http://www.newsweek.com/2010/05/27/reading-ranting-and-arithmetic.html.

Dixon, T., and C. Azocar. 2007. "Priming Crime and Activating Blackness: Understanding the Psychological Impact of Blacks as Lawbreakers on Television News." *Journal of Communication* 57 (2): 229–53.

Domke, D., K. McCoy, and M. Torres. 1999. "News Media, Racial Perceptions, and Political Cognition." *Communication Research* 26 (5): 570–607.

Doob, A. N., and G. E. Macdonald. 1979. "Television Viewing and Fear of Victimization: Is the Relationship Causal?" *Journal of Personality and Social Psychology* 37 (2): 170.

Drier, H., and N. Tabak. 2009. "Cable News Caricatures Immigration Issue with Ubiquitous Footage of Border Crossers." *Media Matters,* 16 April. http:// mediamatters.org/research/2009/04/16/cable-news-caricatures-immigration -issue-with-u/149255.

Edelman, M. 1964. *The Symbolic Uses of Politics.* Champaign: University of Illinois Press.

Elfrink, T. 2010. "Florida's Arizona-Style Immigration Bill Would Give Canadians, Europeans a Free Pass." *Miami New Times,* 18 October. http://blogs.miaminew times.com/riptide/2010/10/floridas_arizona-style_immigra.php.

Entman, R. 1990. "Modern Racism and the Images of Blacks in Local Television News." *Critical Studies in Mass Communication* 7:332–45.

———. 1994. "Representation and Reality in the Portrayal of Blacks on Network Television News." *Journalism Quarterly* 71 (3): 509–20.

Epstein, R. 2014. "National Council of La Raza leader calls Obama 'deporter-in-chief.'" *Politico,* 4 March. http://www.politico.com/story/2014/03/national -council-of-la-raza-janet-murguia-barack-obama-deporter-in-chief-immigration -104217.html.

Esses, V. M., J. F. Dovidio, L. M. Jackson, and T. L. Armstrong. 2001. "The Immigration Dilemma: The Role of Perceived Competition, Ethnic Prejudice, and National Identity." *Journal of Social Issues* 57 (3): 389–412.

Esses, V. M., L. M. Jackson, and T. L. Armstrong. 1998. "Intergroup Competition and Attitudes toward Immigrants and Immigration: An Instrumental Model." *Journal of Social Issues* 54 (3): 699–724.

Extension of the Bracero Program of July 12, 1951. Pub. L. No. 82–78, Stat. 119.

Farley, R. 2017. "No Evidence Sanctuary Cities 'Breed Crime.'" FactCheck.org.

10 February. http://www.factcheck.org/2017/02/no-evidence-sanctuary-cities -breed-crime/.

Fernandez, M., and M. Shear. 2014. "Texas Governor Bolsters Border, and His Profile." *New York Times,* 21 July. http://www.nytimes.com/2014/07/22/us/perry -to-deploy-national-guard-troops-to-mexico-border.html?_r=1.

Fetzer, J. S. 2000. *Public Attitudes toward Immigration in the United States, France, and Germany.* New York: Cambridge University Press.

Foster Global. 2007. *USCIS History of Immigration: Legislation from 1901–1940.* http://www.fosterglobal.com/policy_papers/CISHistoryOfImmigLegislation From1940–1960.pdf.

Fraga, L. 2009. "Building through Exclusion: Anti-Immigrant Politics in the United States." In *Bringing Outsiders In: Transatlantic Perspectives on Immigrant Political Incorporation,* ed. J. Hochschild and J. Mollenkopf, 176–92. Ithaca, NY: Cornell University Press.

Friends of Sharron Angle. 2010. "At Your Expense." Television ad published 23 September. https://www.youtube.com/watch?v=uJC_RmcO7Ts.

Frymer, P., and J. D. Skrentny. 1998. "Coalition-Building and the Politics of Electoral Capture during the Nixon Administration: African Americans, Labor, Latinos." *Studies in American Political Development* 12 (1): 131–61.

Fujioka, Y. 2011. "Perceived Threats and Latino Immigrant Attitudes: How White and African American College Students Respond to News Coverage of Latino Immigrants." *Howard Journal of Communications* 22 (1): 43–63.

Gallup News. 2016. "Immigration." http://www.gallup.com/poll/1660/immigration .aspx.

Garcia, J. 1980. *Operation Wetback: The Mass Deportation of Mexican Undocumented Workers in 1954.* Santa Barbara, CA: Praeger.

Gay, C. 2006. "Seeing Difference: The Effect of Economic Disparity on Black Attitudes toward Latinos." *American Journal of Political Science* 50 (4): 982–97.

Gilliam, F. D., Jr., and S. Iyengar. 2000. "Prime Suspects: The Influence of Local Television News on the Viewing Public." *American Journal of Political Science* 44 (3): 560–73.

Glaeser, E. L., and J. L. Vigdor. 2001. *Racial Segregation in the 2000 Census: Promising News.* Washington, DC: Brookings Institution, Center on Urban and Metropolitan Policy.

Gonzalez, D. 2013. "Deportations by the federal government drop in 2013." *USA Today,* 27 December. http://www.usatoday.com/story/news/nation/2013/12/27 /federal-government-deportations-decrease/4216797/.

Gonzalez O'Brien, B., L. Collingwood, and S. El-Khatib. 2017. "The Politics of Refuge: Sanctuary Cities, Crime, and Undocumented Immigration." *Urban Affairs Review.* http://journals.sagepub.com/doi/abs/10.1177/1078087417704974 ?journalCode=uarb.

Gusfeld, J. 1981. *The Culture of Public Problems.* Chicago: University of Chicago Press.

Hamlin, R. 2015. "Ideology, International Law, and the INS: The Development of American Asylum Politics, 1948–Present." *Polity* 47 (3): 320–36.

Henry, P. J., and D. O. Sears. 2002. "The Symbolic Racism 2000 Scale." *Political Psychology* 23 (2): 253–83.

Hernandez, K. L. 2010. *Migra! A History of the US Border Patrol.* Berkeley: University of California Press.

Herrnstein, R., and C. Murray. 1994. *The Bell Curve: Intelligence and Class Structure in American Life.* New York: Free Press.

Higham, J. 1994. *Strangers in the Land: Patterns of American Nativism, 1860–1925.* New York: Atheneum.

Hoffman, A. 1974. *Unwanted Mexican Americans in the Great Depression: Repatriation Pressures, 1929–1939.* Tucson: University of Arizona Press.

Holmes, S. A. 1995. "Surprising Rise in Immigration Stirs Up Debate." *New York Times,* 30 August.

Huber, G. A., and J. S. Lapinski. 2006. "The 'Race Card' Revisited: Assessing Racial Priming in Policy Contests." *American Journal of Political Science* 50 (2): 421–40.

Ignatiev, N. 1995. *How the Irish Became White.* New York: Routledge.

Immigration Act of March 4th, 1929. Pub. L. No. 1018, Stat. 1551.

Immigration Act of May 26th, 1924. Pub. L. No. 68–139, Stat. 153.

Immigration and Nationality Act of October 3, 1965. Pub. L. No. 89–236, Stat. 911.

Immigration and Nationality Act Amendments of October 20, 1976. Pub. L. No. 94–571, Stat. 2703.

Immigration Reform and Control Act of 1986. Pub. L. No. 99–603, Stat. 3359.

Inda, J. 2008. *Targeting Immigrants: Government, Technology, and Ethics.* John Wiley & Sons.

Iyengar, S., and D. Kinder. 1987. *News That Matters: Agenda-Setting and Priming in a Television Age.* Chicago: University of Chicago Press.

Iyengar, S., and A. Simon. 1993. "News Coverage of the Gulf Crisis and Public Opinion: A Study of Agenda-Setting, Priming, and Framing." *Communication Research* 20 (3): 365–83.

Jacobson, M. F. 1998. *Whiteness of a Different Color: European Immigrants and the Alchemy of Race.* Cambridge, MA: Harvard University Press.

Jacobson, R. D. 2008. *The New Nativism: Proposition 187 and the Debate over Immigration.* Minneapolis: University of Minnesota Press.

Johnson, D. M. 2001. "The AEDPA and the IIRIRA: Treating Misdemeanors as Felonies for Immigration Purposes." *Journal of Legislation* 27 (2): 477–92.

Kanstroom, D. 2007. *Deportation Nation: Outsiders in American History.* Cambridge, MA: Harvard University Press.

Kerr, B., W. Miller, and M. Reid. 2000. "The Changing Face of Urban Bureaucracy: Is There Inter-Ethnic Competition for Municipal Government Jobs?" *Urban Affairs Review* 35:770–93.

Kim, S., J. Carvalho, A. Davis, and A. Mullins. 2011. "The View of the Border: News, Framing of the Definition, Causes, and Solutions to Illegal Immigration." *Mass Communication* 14:292–314.

Kopan, T. 2016. "What Trump has said about Mexico and vice versa." CNN Politics. 31 August. http://www.cnn.com/2016/08/31/politics/donald-trump-mexico-statements/.

Kulish, N., C. Dickerson, and R. Robbins. 2017. "Reports of Raids Have Immigrants Bracing for Enforcement Surge." *New York Times,* 10 February. https://www.nytimes.com/2017/02/10/us/immigration-raids-enforcement.html?_r=0.

Lee, M. T., R. Martinez, and R. Rosenfeld. 2001. "Does Immigration Increase Homicide?" *Sociological Quarterly* 42 (4): 559–80.

Lee, Y.-T., and V. Ottati. 2002. "Attitudes toward U.S. Immigration Policy: The Roles of In-Group–Out-Group Bias, Economic Concern, and Obedience to Law." *Journal of Social Psychology* 142 (5): 617–34.

Lippmann, W. 1922. *Public Opinion.* Sioux Falls, SD: Greenbook.

Logan, J. 2001. *Ethnic Diversity Grows, Neighborhood Integration Lags Behind.* Albany: Lewis Mumford Center, State University of New York.

Lyons, C., M. Velez, and W. Santoro. 2013. "Neighborhood Immigration, Violence, and City-Level Immigrant Political Opportunities." *American Sociological Review* 78 (4): 604–32.

Maio, G. R., V. M. Esses, and D. W. Bell. 1994. "The Formation of Attitudes toward New Immigrant Groups." *Journal of Applied Social Psychology* 24: 1762–76.

Martinez, R., and M. Lee. 2000. "On Immigration and Crime." In *The Nature of Crime: Continuity and Change.* Vol. 1 of *Criminal Justice 2000.* Washington, DC: US Department of Justice. https://www.ncjrs.gov/criminal_justice2000/vol1_2000.html.

Martinez, R., J. Stowell, and M. Lee. 2010. "Immigration and Crime in an Era of Transformation: A Longitudinal Analysis of Homicides in San Diego Neighborhoods, 1980–2000." *Criminology* 48 (3): 797–829.

Massey, D. S. 2007. *Categorically Unequal: The American Stratification System.* New York: Russell Sage Foundation.

Massey, D. S., and A. Singer. 1995. "New Estimates of Undocumented Mexican Migration and the Probability of Apprehension." *Demography* 32 (2): 203–13.

Masuoka, N., and J. Junn. 2013. *The Politics of Belonging: Race, Public Opinion, and Immigration.* Chicago: University of Chicago Press.

Mendelberg, T. 2001. *The Race Card: Campaign Strategy, Implicit Messages, and the Norm of Equality.* Princeton, NJ: Princeton University Press.

Merica, D. 2015. "Bill Clinton says he made mass incarceration issue worse." CNN Politics. 15 July.http://www.cnn.com/2015/07/15/politics/bill-clinton-1994-crime-bill/.

———. 2017. "Trump signs executive order to keep out 'radical Islamic terrorists.'" CNN Politics. 30 January. http://www.cnn.com/2017/01/27/politics/trump-plans-to-sign-executive-action-on-refugees-extreme-vetting/index.html.

Merolla, J., K. Ramakrishnan, and C. Haynes. 2013. "'Illegal,' 'Undocumented,' or 'Unauthorized': Equivalency Frames, Issue Frames, and Public Opinion on Immigration." *Perspectives on Politics* 11 (3): 789–807.

Milbank, D. 2010. "Headless bodies and other tall tales in Arizona." *Washington Post,* 9 July. http://www.washingtonpost.com/wp-dyn/content/article/2010/07/09/AR2010070902342.html.

Miller, T. A. 2003. "Citizenship and Severity: Recent Immigration Reforms and the New Penology." *Georgetown Immigration Law Journal* 17 (4): 611–66.

Muller, T. 1994. *Immigrants and the American City.* New York: New York University Press.

National Commission on Law Observance and Enforcement (NCLOE). 1931. *Report on Crime and the Foreign Born.* Washington, DC: Government Printing Office.

Nevins, J. 2010. *Operation Gatekeeper: The Rise of the "Illegal Alien" and the Making of the U.S.-Mexico Boundary.* New York: Routledge.

Newton, L. 2008. *Illegal, Alien, or Immigrant: The Politics of Immigration Reform.* New York: New York University Press.

Ngai, M. M. 1999. "The Architecture of Race in American Immigration Policy: A Reexamination of the Immigration Act of 1924." *Journal of American History* 86 (1): 67–92.

———. 2003. "The Strange Career of the Illegal Alien: Immigration Restriction and Deportation Policy in the United States, 1921–1965." *Law and History Review* 21 (1): 69–108.

———. 2004. *Impossible Subjects: Illegal Aliens and the Making of Modern America.* Princeton, NJ: Princeton University Press.

Nteta, T. 2013. "United We Stand? African Americans, Self-Interest, and Immigration Reform." *American Politics Research* 41 (1): 147–72.

———. 2014. "The Past is Prologue: African American Opinion toward Undocumented Immigration." *Social Science History* 38 (3): 389–410.

Office of Hillary Rodham Clinton. 2016. "Immigration Reform." https://www.hillaryclinton.com/issues/immigration-reform/.

Orren, K., and S. Skowronek. 2004. *The Search for American Political Development.* Cambridge: Cambridge University Press.

Padgett, T. 2010. "The 'Dangerous' Border: Actually One of America's Safest Places." *Time,* 30 July. http://www.time.com/time/nation/article/0,8599,2007474,00.html.

Peffley, M., T. Shields, and B. Williams. 1996. "The Intersection of Race and Crime in Television News Stories: An Experimental Study." *Political Communication* 13 (3): 309–27.

Pew Research Center. 2012. "Majority Approves of Arizona Immigration Law." 21 June. http://www.pewresearch.org/daily-number/majority-approves-of-arizona-immigration-law/.

———. 2014. "Record Number of Deportations in 2012." 24 January. http://www.pewresearch.org/fact-tank/2014/01/24/record-number-of-deportations-in-2012/.

Pew Research Hispanic Trends Project. 2013. "US Unauthorized Immigration Population Trends, 1990–2012." 23 September. http://www.pewhispanic.org/2013/09/23/unauthorized-trends/#All.

Pierson, P. 2000. "Increasing Returns, Path Dependence, and the Study of Politics." *American Political Science Review* 94 (2): 251–67.

———. 2004. *Politics in Time: History, Institutions, and Social Analysis.* Princeton, NJ: Princeton University Press.

PollingReport.com. 2016a. "Health Policy." http://www.pollingreport.com/health.htm.

————. 2016b. "Immigration." http://www.pollingreport.com/immigration.htm.

Porter, E. 2005. "Illegal Immigrants are Bolstering Social Security with Billions." *New York Times,* 5 April.

Pratto, F., and A. F. Lemieux. 2001. "The Psychological Ambiguity of Immigration and Its Implications for Promoting Immigration Policy." *Journal of Social Issues* 57 (3): 413–30.

Pratto, F., J. Sidanius, L. M. Stallworth, and B. F. Malle. 1994. "Social Dominance Orientation: A Personality Variable Predicting Social and Political Attitudes." *Journal of Personality and Social Psychology* 67 (4): 741–63.

Prior, M. 2007. *Post-Broadcast Democracy: How Media Choice Increases Inequality in Political Involvement and Polarizes Elections.* Cambridge: Cambridge University Press.

Provine, D., and R. Doty. 2011. "The Criminalization of Immigrants as Racial Project." *Journal of Contemporary Criminal Justice* 27 (3): 261–77.

Quillian, L. 1995. "Prejudice as a Response to Perceived Group Threat: Population Composition and Anti-Immigrant and Racial Prejudice in Europe." *American Sociological Review* 60 (4): 596–611.

Quillian, L., and D. Pager. 2010. "Estimating Risk: Stereotype Amplification and the Perceived Risk of Criminal Victimization." *Social Psychology Quarterly* 73 (1): 79–104.

Rasmussen Reports. 2015. "Voters Want to Punish Sanctuary Cities." 10 July. http://www.rasmussenreports.com/public_content/politics/current_events /immigration/july_2015/voters_want_to_punish_sanctuary_cities.

Raynar, R. 1996. "What Immigration Crisis?" *New York Times Magazine,* 7 January. http://www.nytimes.com/1996/01/07/magazine/what-immigration-crisis .html?pagewanted=all.

Restriction of Western Hemisphere Immigration: Hearings before the Committee on Immigration, United States Senate. 1928. 70th Congress.

Ridgley, J. 2008. "Cities of Refuge: Immigration Enforcement, Police, and the Insurgent Genealogies of Citizenship in U.S. Sanctuary Cities." *Urban Geography* 29 (1): 53–77.

Romer, D., K. H. Jamieson, and S. Aday. 2003) "Television News and the Cultivation of Fear of Crime." *Journal of Communication* 53 (1): 88–104.

Russell-Brown, K. 1998. *The Color of Crime: Racial Hoaxes, White Fear, Black Protectionism, Police Harassment and Other Microaggressions.* New York: New York University Press.

Sanchez, A. 2010. "Jan Brewer Falsely Claims Undocumented Immigrants Come to US to Bring Drugs, Extort, and Terrorize." Think Progress. 24 June. http:// thinkprogress.org/politics/2010/06/24/104445/jan-brewer-crime/.

Santa Ana, O. 2002. *Brown Tide Rising: Metaphors of Latinos in Contemporary American Public Discourse.* Austin: University of Texas Press.

————. 2013. *Juan in a Hundred: The Representation of Latinos on Network News.* Austin: University of Texas Press.

Schemer, C. 2012. "The Influence of News Media on Stereotypic Attitudes toward Immigrants in a Political Campaign." *Journal of Communication* 62 (5): 739–57.

Scheufele, D. A. 2000. "Agenda-Setting, Priming, and Framing Revisited: Another Look at Cognitive Effects of Political Communication." *Mass Communication and Society* 3 (2–3): 297–316.

Scheufele, D. A., and D. Tewksbury. 2007. "Framing, Agenda Setting, and Priming: The Evolution of Three Media Effects Models." *Journal of Communication* 57 (1): 9–20.

Schnell, K. C. F. 2001. "Assessing the Democratic Debate: How the News Media Frame Elite Policy Discourse." *Political Communication* 18 (2): 183–213.

Schreckinger, B. 2015. "White supremacist groups see Trump bump." *Politico,* 10 December.

Sewell, W. H., Jr. 2005. *Logics of History: Social Theory and Social Transformation.* Chicago: University of Chicago Press.

Sidanius, J. 1993. "The Psychology of Group Conflict and the Dynamics of Oppression: A Social Dominance Perspective." In *Explorations in Political Psychology,* ed. S. Iyengar and W. McGuire, 183–219. Durham, NC: Duke University Press.

Sidanius, J., and F. Pratto. 2001. *Social Dominance: An Intergroup Theory of Social Hierarchy and Oppression.* Cambridge: Cambridge University Press.

Simon, B. 1996. "The Appeal of Cole Blease of South Carolina: Race, Class, and Sex in the New South." *Journal of Southern History* 62 (1): 57–86.

Simon, J. 2001. "Sanctioning Government: Explaining America's Severity Revolution." *University of Miami Law Review* 56 (1): 217–53.

———. 2007. *Governing through Crime: How the War on Crime Transformed American Democracy and Created a Culture of Fear.* Oxford: Oxford University Press.

Smith, R. M. 1993. "Beyond Tocqueville, Myrdal, and Hartz: The Multiple Traditions in America." *American Political Science Review* 87 (3): 549–66.

Sniderman, P. M., L. Hagendoorn, and M. Prior. 2004. "Predisposing Factors and Situational Triggers: Exclusionary Reactions to Immigrant Minorities." *American Political Science Review* 98 (1): 35–49.

Stephan, W., C. Renfro, V. Esses, C. Stephan, and T. Martin. 2005. "The Effects of Feeling Threatened on Attitudes toward Immigrants." *International Journal of Intercultural Relations* 29:1–19.

Stephan, W., O. Ybarra, and G. Bachman. 1999. "Prejudice toward Immigrants." *Journal of Applied Social Psychology* 29 (11): 2221–37.

Stevens, R. 2016. *Immigration Policy from 1970 to the Present.* New York: Routledge.

Stone, D. 1989. "Causal Stories and the Formation of Policy Agendas." *Political Science Quarterly* 104 (2): 281–300.

Stumpf, J. P. 2006. "The Crimmigration Crisis: Immigrants, Crime, and Sovereign Power." *American University Law Review* 56 (2): 367–419.

Thelan, K. 1999. "Historical Institutionalism in Comparative Politics." *Annual Review of Political Science* 2:369–404.

Tichenor, D. 2002. *Dividing Lines: The Politics of Immigration in America.* Princeton, NJ: Princeton University Press.

Trump, D. J. 2016a. Acceptance speech to Republican National Convention,

21 July, Cincinnati, OH. https://www.politico.com/story/2016/07/full
-transcript-donald-trump-nomination-acceptance-speech-at-rnc-225974.
————. 2016b. "Healthcare Reform to Make America Great Again." http://amc
trump.org/2016/03/05/8/.
US Commission on Immigration. 1911. *Reports of the Immigration Commission: Immigration and Crime.* Washington, DC: Government Printing Office.
US Commission on Immigration Reform. 1994. *U.S. Immigration Policy: Restoring Credibility.* Washington, DC: Government Printing Office.
US Immigration and Customs Enforcement. 2015. *ICE Enforcement and Removal Operations Report, Fiscal Year 2015.* Washington, DC: US Department of Homeland Security. https://www.ice.gov/sites/default/files/documents/Report /2016/fy2015removalStats.pdf.
US Senate Committee on Immigration. 1929. *Making it a felony with penalty for certain aliens to enter the United States of American under certain conditions in violation of the law (to accompany S. 5094).* 70 S. Rpt. 1456. Text from *Committee Reports.*
Uwimana, S. 2011. *Report: In Immigration Coverage, Fox Shuns Pro-Immigrant Voices.* http://mediamatters.org/research/2011/10/27/report-in-immigration -coverage-fox-shuns-pro-im/183143.
Valentino, N. A., T. Brader, and A. E. Jardina. 2013. "Immigration Opposition among US Whites: General Ethnocentrism or Media Priming of Attitudes about Latinos?" *Political Psychology* (2): 149–66.
Violent Crime Control and Law Enforcement Act of 1994. Pub. L. No. 103–322, Stat. 1796.
Vobejda, B. 1992. "Births, Immigration Revise Census View of 21st Century US." *Washington Post,* 4 December.
Wadsworth, T. 2010. "Is Immigration Responsible for the Crime Drop? An Assessment of the Influence of Immigration on Changes in Violent Crime between 1990 and 2000." *Social Science Quarterly* 91 (3): 531–53.
Warren, R., and J. S. Passel. 1987. "A Count of the Uncountable: Estimates of Undocumented Aliens Counted in the 1980 United States Census." *Demography* 24 (3): 375–93.
Wasem, R. E. 2012. "Unauthorized Aliens Residing in the United States: Estimates since 1986." *Congressional Research Service,* 13 December.
Welch, K. 2007. "Black Criminal Stereotypes and Racial Profiling." *Journal of Contemporary Criminal Justice* 23 (3): 276–88.
"White House Call the Shots, As Illegal Alien Bill Clears." 1996. *CQ Almanac.* https://library.cqpress.com/cqalmanac/document.php?id=cqal96–1092264.
Wilson, T. C. 2001. "Americans' View on Immigration Policy: Testing the Role of Threatened Group Interests." *Sociological Perspectives* 44 (4): 485–501.
Yee, V., K. Davis, and J. Patel. 2017. "Here's the Reality about Illegal Immigrants in the United States." *New York Times,* 6 March. https://www.nytimes.com /interactive/2017/03/06/us/politics/undocumented-illegal-immigrants.html ?mcubz=3&_r=0.

Zaller, J. 1992. *The Nature and Origins of Mass Opinion.* Cambridge: Cambridge University Press.

Zaller, J., and D. Chiu. 1996. "Government's Little Helper: US Press Coverage of Foreign Policy Crises, 1945–1991." *Political Communication* 13 (4): 385–405.

Zarate, M., B. Garcia, A. Garza, and R. Hitlan. 2004. "Cultural Threat and Perceived Realistic Group Conflict as Dual Predictors of Prejudice." *Journal of Experimental Social Psychology* 40:99–105.

Zolberg, A. R. 2006. *A Nation by Design: Immigration Policy in the Fashioning of America.* Cambridge, MA: Harvard University Press.

INDEX